Barry J. Gibbons

This Indecision is FINAL

32 management secrets of
Albert Einstein, Billie Holiday,
and a bunch of other people
who never worked 9 to 5

IRWIN
Professional Publishing®
Chicago • London • Singapore

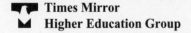 **Times Mirror**
Higher Education Group

Library of Congress Cataloging-in-Publication Data

Gibbons, Barry J.
    This indecision is final : 32 management secrets of Billie
Holliday, Albert Einstein, and a bunch of other people who never
worked 9 to 5 / Barry J. Gibbons.
        p.   cm.
    ISBN 0-7863-0838-9
    1. Management.   I. Title.
HD31.G4918   1996
658—dc20   95–51784

Printed in the United States of America
1 2 3 4 5 6 7 8 9 0 XX 2 1 0 9 8 7 6 5

This Indecision is FINAL:
Cast (in order of appearance)

Michael Jackson	Alexander the Great
Lisa Marie Presley	Margaret Thatcher
Paul McCartney	Snoop Doggy Dog
Mrs. Paul McCartney	Bob Dylan
Bill and Hillary Clinton	Hugh Grant
Gary Player	Marilyn Monroe
Lee Trevino	John F. Kennedy
Jack Nicklaus	The Dalai Lama
Arnold Palmer	Richard Gere
Gandhi	Tammy Faye Bakker
Kurt Cobain	Boutros Boutros Ghali
Yuri Gagarin	Oliver North
Pope John Paul the Bestseller	Jane Fonda
Mao Ze-Dong	Queen Elizabeth the Second
Grace Kelly	Whoopi Goldberg
Eric Clapton	Harrison Ford
Albert Einstein	Dr. Jacob Bronowski
Luciano Pavarotti	Cat Stevens
Billie Holiday	John Sebastian
Field Marshal Montgomery	Princess 'Fergie'
Wayne Huizenga	Emma Thompson
Salman Rushdie	Kenneth Brannagh
Meg Ryan	Nelson Mandela
James Taylor	Julio Iglesias

Author's Foreword: The essays in this book cover the various dimensions of my relationships with all of the above. Some are just as ships passing, others are deep, meaningful, and lifelong. All have one thing in common: **I have never actually met, or spoken to, anybody on this list.**

Or, to put it another way (that my publisher, whom I think is located on the planet Sporg, would very much like me to): **Any references to identifiable people or entities contained in the book are solely my creation, and are not based on facts or any actual experiences.**

Their unwitting collaboration will not be in vain. It is my intention that the publication of this book will advance civilization, bring peace on Earth and increase the wealth of all nations. All my personal goals are purely subsidiary to that. Absolutely.

B.J.G.

Preface

If you are in the world of business, it is a certainty you are confused. If you love somebody in business, or are the parent or offspring of—or just related to or friendly with—somebody in business, you are likely to be more so.

You haven't figured out the difference between leadership and management. Mistakes and failures are all the same to you. Reengineering seems a good idea, but then how do you handle a pissed-off workforce? Why is it assumed that good communicating is all about transmitting—and not about receiving—information? Just why did the world submerge under a sea of ho-hum products and services? And can the Dalai Lama play a role in fixing things?

Whoa there! Here I am pulling away from the gate, and the wheels are already spinning too fast. I need you to forget the Dalai Lama (for a while). I need you to think about a Swiss army knife.

It's no good going to the bookstore to ease the confusion about business. God, no. Acres of space, miles of shelving, and thousands of titles (it seems) are designed to add to your bewilderment. There's big money in the status quo.

Oh, for the business book equivalent of a Swiss army knife: a compendium of useful tools in a single unit, designed to fit in your pocket and armed with which you can take on anything.

And you wondered why Hitler left Switzerland alone?

Nothing less grand is my goal in this series of thirty-something essays written over the last couple of years. If you figure in the first paragraph of this preface, they are written with you in mind. If you are an "also-ran" or a "wannabe," or a "has been" or a "never was," they are for you. Everything's here, from the business equal of the tiny nail scissors to the odd-looking thing they use for punching holes in their otherwise nondescript cheese.

Wow. Sounds impressive.

So how does the Dalai Lama figure in this?

When a company moves from a functional headquarters to something palatial, the stock price is likely to spend some time in the toilet. So says the handed-down wisdom of generations of market makers. My company did, and it did—but that is somebody else's story. The opulent new boardroom played a bit part in shaping this.

In 1989 the UK-based Grand Metropolitan PLC (GrandMet) completed the contested acquisition of the US food giant Pillsbury (which included Burger King Corporation among the lesser jewels in its portfolio). I was with GrandMet in England, and with a reasoning that still confuses me, they offered me the job of CEO of Burger King. With a reasoning that confuses me even more, I accepted and moved to Miami. Yes, Miami.

This is not the story of my five years there, nor is it any kind of Burger King story; neither of those sagas will be written by me. Life is simply too short to dedicate big chunks of it to masturbation or flatulence, and both would be rampant in such a work.

But Burger King was the last 5 of 25 years in big business, during which I have seen things and been influenced. I have done some things and tried some others, shaping my views accordingly. The results are not in this book; they *are* this book.

I've had a couple of epiphanies on the way, one of which was definitely in the last five years.

GrandMet rapidly added business value to its troubled new acquisitions, but there were cultural missteps along the way, particularly in the field of what Americans have defined as *diversity*, to which they (generally) accord much higher profile and sensitivity.

A workshop was needed at the highest level, and the Group Operating Committee duly assembled from their various global bases. Jet-lagged and unconvinced, we met under the crystal chandeliers of the new boardroom to "Star Trek" this complex subject: to boldly go where no one has gone before. Or should that be to boldly split infinitives . . .

It is a universal rule that leaders eventually believe their own publicity and begin to parody themselves. The self-confidence that was nutritional on your journey to the top wakes up one morning as an ego that is corrosive. You're usually the last to see it.

> It is a universal rule that all leaders eventually believe their own publicity and begin to parody themselves.

It was happening to me, and I knew it. I did not want to be in this meeting. Diversity issues in Burger King were material, but the company had got into a mess through evolution and was not going to get out by revolution. What we had in place was a program of fast evolution to address the core problems, and I was happy with that, given the other mild distraction we had of staying alive in the market. The last thing I wanted was some central staffer imposing a slow-down/speed-up directive on Burger King based on the outcome of the group workshop.

We had an outside facilitator, and the process started slowly. We picked up speed in a session that involved us all talking about our own discriminations, based on the unassailable logic that we've all got 'em.

I have low boredom threshold, and sailed over it early on, but the irony of what we were doing kept me awake. I have an MBA from one of England's most prestigious business schools but had spent most of my corporate life trying to unlearn the theories I digested in school, in the face of the practicalities of making the next set of published results look good. Here we were taking it one step further. Here, a group of unbelievably well-paid guys with high intellects were discussing how they could re-create a second childhood for themselves, their organizations, and their employees. How they could put in place policies and procedures to combat the bigotry, fear, distaste, paranoia, insensitivity, and rank discourtesy that you are born without, but pick up on the way like chewing gum on the soles of your shoes?

I played with the idea for 15 minutes or so and confess I was round the dark side of the moon as far as the meeting was concerned. I came back just as one of my colleagues was giving a speech about men wearing earrings. I think he was suggesting they should be lethally injected or have their balls cut off. Such men certainly weren't going to work any place where *he* was responsible for painting the wagons.

It's difficult to pinpoint exactly when a midlife crisis starts. Like a tropical rainstorm in Florida, guys will tell you that you can often see it before you drive into it, but the exact moment of entry is hard to record. Later that evening, I was scrambling round my suburban home looking for something—anything—that I could use as an earring for the next day's session. I eventually found a key ring, and that's as good a moment as any to signal the start of mine.

The rest is history. My midlife crisis is in its fifth year, and I love it. I dread its ending.

I wore the "earring" in the hallowed halls the next day, complete with an IBM-type suit, shirt, and tie. I felt as though my fly was undone. Rather disappointingly, nobody batted an eyelid—apart, that is, from the empty suit who gave the original speech who recorded one of the greatest Hollywood-style double takes of all time when he saw it. That alone was worth the price of admission.

My two sons never batted an eyelid, although the youngest (very) helpfully pointed out that I was wearing the earring on the side that indicated a sexual preference that he assumed wasn't mine. I changed that, and my sons were enormously entertained from then on.

Some other results:

- My marriage suffered, then we astonished ourselves.

- My approach to leadership both suffered and thrived, depending on your vantage point.

- I invented a "test of rightness" for everything I and the company were doing, and for what every leader and every company I could see or read about were doing. The average score was about 4 out of 10 on a good day, with some cheating.

- My corporate ambition imploded. Correction: When I went looking for it, I found I didn't have any. Twenty-five years of promotion after promotion in big business had seen me on the front of *Fortune* magazine and running one of the world's high profile brands, but all I'd done was to say "yes" when somebody offered me the next job. I'd received more money, more responsibility, more status, more stuff.

I'd never contemplated an alternative, I didn't know there was an alternative. Smell the roses on the way? Guys like me have their noses surgically removed. If it's not about the next quarter, forget it.

At the end of 1993, after working out a handover process with GrandMet, I quit. I was a free man, with absolutely no idea what was next.

I remain capitalist through and through. I believe in enlightened free enterprise and wealth creation as the best way of addressing the planet's complexities, principally because nothing else works. I also believe that business is not enlightened and that it is generally run by myopic and paranoid people, with a few glorious exceptions.

> Business is not enlightened. It is generally run by myopic and paranoid people.

My father was from County Cork. Irish blood runs deep in my veins and is thickening with the years. I have always loved the spoken and written word, and the juxta-position of the serious and the bizarre. My adolescence in the north of England added an acerbic sense of humor. I developed a public speaking style for business that com-bined all these influences in a rather absurd cocktail, the demand for which grew as I signaled the end of my day-to-day involvement in big company life. Work that out.

As I began to shape my material, these essays crystallized.

Speaking of the Dalai Lama (and I will), I learned to love communication and information technology from the moment I lost my fear of both. Through the wonders of digital remixing, I'm fascinated by watching a movie in which Tom Hanks seemingly meets and converses with historic figures.

It seemed the only limit on digitally remixing my essays in a similar way was my sense of the absurd and potential litigation. Neither has proved a barrier (so far). Why not develop my relationship with Billie Holliday to see what she could offer on the subject of diversity? With Field Marshal Montgomery on leadership? With Einstein for training and motivation?

Welcome to Aesop meets Forrest Gump, the corporate edition.

Barry Gibbons
Gibbonfile @ aol.com
Florida, 1996

Contents

Section 1 2 3 4 5

Power to the People

Yeah, right **33**

Section 1 2 **3** 4 5

Leadership and Management

I will follow you if you'll follow me   **67**

Section 1 2 3 **4** 5

Organizations—and Organizing

To be or not to be?   **103**

Section 1 2 3 4 5

Doing Things Differently

1

Impacting the Marketplace

Or, how to avoid banging on the window with a sponge

Introduction

Surgeon General's health warning: Beware of this section. It is written by a guy who invented, launched, and oversaw the rapid demise of a retail brand called—wait for it—*Death in the Afternoon.* ∎

It's true. The seventies saw an explosion in demand for wine bars in England. I had a fabulous property available in the heart of a provincial city and set about creating a wine bar with the enthusiasm that comes only from true greed.

Death in the Afternoon was to be its name and it boded a breakthrough in British branding. If you've ever lingered too long over wine at lunchtime, you'll know that such a "death" is precisely what's ahead of you about four o'clock. The name also enabled me to theme the place with wonderful Hemingway-style imagery from bullfighting. I couldn't wait to open one of these bars, then the second, then the tenth, then the hundredth, and so on.

By the end of the second operating week, by which time we were nearly ready to open our *second* bottle of wine, I knew I had a failure and closed the doors. The customers made it clear they wanted names like *Cork and Bottle,* and that they didn't want sepia images of dead bulls.

I learned a lot from that bomb. You don't impact the market by pursuing your own ego and cleverness. Marketing masturbation is a personal thing. Not many others want to be involved.

What does work is to spot a gap in the market and to drive a truck into it.

Gap spotting is a rare talent, probably God-given, and I haven't got it. Richard Branson, the Virgin king, has it by the bucketful. In later years, however, I proved to be a good truck driver.

The world, with two exceptions, believes prostitution to be the oldest profession. Marlon Brando believes it to be acting. I believe it is branding. Both prostitution and acting are but two of its (many, many) derivatives.

Branding is the key to marketplace impact for any product or service, but it is not just about a familiar-looking packet of soap powder. Elvis was (is?) a brand, and so is your credit card, church, laundry detergent, and insurance company. So too is just about everything else that makes up your world.

Distinction is what gets marketplace impact, and as there is no finer one-word definition of branding. Distinction and branding are one and the same to me. It is not about being better or worse, cheaper or more expensive.

Growing up in Europe, I saw two perfectly positioned car brands.

- Rolls Royce: If you even questioned the maintenance costs, you probably couldn't afford it.
- Volkswagen: Simply the cheapest way to get on the road.

Every other brand was somewhere in between and, therefore, less distinct—and less effective.

The last decade has seen branding evolve. The recession that bit so deeply made customers—both retail or wholesale buyers of products and services—much more savvy. The previous affluent decades had seen business and personal risks underpinned by asset inflation and personal and business security. Sloppy practices became the order of the day, particularly in buying. It was too easy for the brand owner: Much distinction became based on bullshit.

> **Distinction is what gets marketplace impact.**

Many companies have now reengineered their whole approach to procurement. Consumers live in a world of increasing job insecurity and asset deflation. When these folks buy anything today, bullshit don't work no more.

The value era is here. This does not mean distinction by price is your only avenue. It means getting your product and/or service to the market with a high impact combination of quality, price, and service relationship. The latter reflects every dimension of the relationship between you and your customer. That's what makes for value today.

Oh, yeah. Something else: You can't rely on *perceived* value anymore; it's a house of cards. Value *reality* is what counts. And today's buyers just seem to know it when they see it.

In my years on the planet, and my fewer years in business, I have been exposed to thousands (millions?) of statistics. Most went in one orifice and out of another. Some stayed around awhile. Three of them hit me like heat-seeking missiles:

- It is estimated that Africa lost 50 million of its people to American slavery.
- In the developed world, we acquire 90% of what we personally own for effect.
- Between 70% and 90% of decisions not to repeat a purchase of anything are not about product or price. They are about some dimension of the service relationship.

Two of these statistics have nothing to do with impacting the marketplace. One has *everything* to do with it. For those of you who've never managed to hit this one on the sweet spot, the answer is somewhere in there. The seven essays in this section kick it around a bit.

1

On Brands

And the benefits of moonwalking

Provided we can all contain our excitement, I want to start the discussion on branding. Recently, I attended a wedding that raised in my mind many of the issues involved in branding. This was a particularly big (but hush-hush) event, as my mentee of many years ago, Michael Jackson, pledged his troth to his lovely bride, Lisa Marie Presley. Naturally, he asked me along as best man.

> *(For the benefit of any readers interested in this kind of information, I am able to report that Lisa looked lovely in white as she stood, looking demure and thoughtful, in front of the Judge. For the benefit of any readers otherwise interested, I can tell you that I, too, would look thoughtful if I were about to marry Michael Jackson.)*

Distinction is the core of branding. Not better or worse. Not cheaper or more expensive; *distinct.* And when you think of Michael Jackson not as a rock star but as one of the great modern brand names—just as you do of

Kelloggs, Tide, American Express, the Dallas Cowboys, the Queen Of England, Microsoft Windows, Coca Cola, your local school or church (in their own local markets), and Sony—you realize that he is about as distinct, in his market, as you can get. Is he ever.

But aren't these just a few examples of brands in a world where most goods and services are distinguishable only by price? A world where the death of brand distinction was signaled on Marlboro Friday in 1992, when Phillip Morris cut the price of its famous brand to stem the loss of market share to unbranded, cheaper cigarettes?

What a crock. I don't want to mince words here, but if you believe that you should either resign and/or sell your business. Now. Do everyone a favor.

Sure you need to compete on price, because price is an integral element of the customer's definition of value. But so too are product consistency and performance. And so too are service and the relationship that can, and should, be part of your brand package, which can appear at the wholesale or retail level. Or both. And by the way, remember *you* determine the importance of each part in the mix.

Yeah, yeah, yeah. Sure there's a drift toward everything becoming a commodity, and everything being determined by price alone, but there's a reason for that drift. It's *easy* to join the Mexican Wave of discounting that is sweeping the Western World, and once you've done that, that's it. You're in there, competing, aren't you? Why would you want to do any more? Discounting has eroded your margins to a degree you *can't* enhance your product or invest in the relationships that accompany it.

So what have we got here? We have a generation of brand owners who were weaned on the milk of the dumbest concept ever to come out of a business school:

Customer Satisfaction. These are brand owners who turn up for work every morning and hang up their flair, guts, creativity, imagination, and commitment on five coat pegs by the door. And, round about 10:30 A.M., slash the sticker price some more.

Customer satisfaction? I wish to make my position quite clear. *We should all spit at customer satisfaction.*

We want to take a company's goods and services, and work with all our resources of price, product, and relationship (notice we don't use the word *service* anymore) and put the customer *in orbit* as a result of using them. I've developed a simple success criterion to take over from customer satisfaction, which is that your customers, having used/experienced your goods/services, will talk about them later—over dinner or with their families. *Then* you can claim distinction. *Then* you have a brand for today and tomorrow.

If that's not your goal, Mr. or Mrs. Brand Owner, prepare to be an also-ran within five years, because that's what modern branding is going to be about. It's not price *or* product *or* relationship, but a mind-blowing cocktail of all three. So what if you run a laundry or a fast-food restaurant prone to mistakes? Or you're the manager of "just another" hotel chain? Or a Mexican restaurant in London that serves pretty ordinary food? Don't tell me you can't ring the bell, because I can give you personal examples of *exactly* those types of brands that got me talking about them later over dinner.

> **I**t's not price *or* product *or* relationship but a mind-blowing cocktail of all three.

Think *orbit*, think *distinction*. And think with your flair, guts, creativity, imagination, and commitment.

Speaking of all those things, our thoughts turn again to Michael. What goes around comes around, and after adding value to the delights of the wedding, I found myself guiding him through the traumas of the divorce. After a suitably appropriate gap in between, of course.

He came down to Florida for my advice and a rather solemn meeting with his lawyers. After we broke up, I watched him as he waved goodbye to me, and then as he pirouetted and moonwalked from the car back to the entrance of the Embassy Suites, where he was staying. The word *distinct* kept running through my head.

Or something like that.

2

On Quality

And problems with personal valets

As many of you know, my mind and body were trained in the jungles just back from Manilla to combat shock in all its forms.

On a recent visit to England, I found myself constantly drawing on this inner strength as I beheld the steady disintegration of my motherland. Witness the fact you now have to ask behind the bar for the bathroom key in many of London's pubs. Witness the ruthless regeneration of some of the provincial cities, turning fine deconstructivist urban decay into dreadful collections of niche retailing concepts.

And witness the savage betrayal, to the tabloids, of Prince Charles by his trusted personal valet—an act that has forced many of us to review the freedoms and newly empowered status of our own valets. I have eight, so it makes my life very difficult.

These were body blows all, you will agree; but all were survived until the final nightmare, which forced me to cut short my visit and scurry for the cultural safe haven of my home in south Miami. I refer, of course, to the publication of the tragic fact that Britain's consumption of caviar fell below four tons last year.

Aghast at the news, my mind wandered back to the halcyon days of the Greedy Capitalist eighties, when a small group of us, jetting between Wall Street and the City of London, would polish off a contested acquisition by midmorning, pocket a couple of hundred million dollars in fees, swell the take with about £60 million of gains from insider trading on the deal, and then disappear to lunch. On our own we would then consume maybe a hundred pounds in weight of Russia's finest export, washed down by heady cocktails of draft Guinness mixed with Dom Perignon. I estimate my own *personal* consumption of caviar to be 2.74 tons in 1986. Quality, quality times, indeed.

They're all over now, of course, but *quality* remains in the corporate dictionary. Today it is defined as a phantom property attributed by many brand marketers to their client's products and/or services, in a keen attempt to penetrate the all-important "customer perception."

The irony is that, delivered properly—that is, the product/service has quality, rather than has it attributed to it, and that it penetrates the customers' *experience*, not their perception—this quality thing can be enormously successful. A thesis along these lines was developed for the West by W. Edwards Deming around 1950, but it was largely rejected on the grounds that quality was much easier to do with mirrors. Unfortunately (for the West) Japan listened and very nearly left us for dead competitively, although some companies have recently twigged and recorded spectacular results. I give you Motorola. Enough said?

Sadly, however, the West remains a universe built on claims of quality rather than delivery, with "ho-hum" being the catch-all description for most products and services—particularly services.

It can appear to be costly and complex to go for the real thing of course. It's one thing for a central unit to, say, brew beer (using a high-tech-controlled process) and to then dispatch it to the customer in a robust package such as a can or bottle. You can be pretty safe in the knowledge that it's going to get there in the shape you want it to. It's quite a different challenge, however, when control of that quality is *distributed*—for example, when that same brewery produces draft beer that requires processing in a local neighborhood bar (frequently, it seems, by aliens). In fast-food chains, actual production of the brand is distributed to hundreds, maybe thousands, of locations.

Get it right, and it works beyond belief. Detailed implementation must differ in detail for every product/service, but I believe there are *six principles* that should be common to all approaches, and if you do all six, you get the seventh for free:

- Quality is not about being cheap or expensive; it's about delivering the agreed specification every time. Define that specification— exactly how the user/buyer should receive your product/service—and *measure* whether that occurs.

- Get the results (good or bad) to those in the organization who need to act on it. Fast.

- Don't celebrate any other figure than 100 percent success (zero defects). Anything else is compromise.

- Everything you do in business life is either *nutritional* or *corrosive*. Quality control must be nutritional; it is not about extra cost, it is about wealth creation. And it should not be ammunition for a "gotcha" blame culture; it's far better to use QC to catch those who do it right and make positive examples.

- Select priorities (or even one big priority) for improvement. Focus works.
- Raise awareness by the only method that is effective: Build personal quality goals into personal objectives. If corporate quality goals are not met, no bonus of any kind gets paid. To anybody. Period.

What about the seventh point? The one you get free if you achieve the above six? Well, you can build these principles into your marketing. Marketing is about the *communication of distinction.* Do all six and your brand will be distinct all right. So will your market share, margins, and cash flow.

> **E**verything you do in business life is either nutritional or corrosive.

If you can get this backbone into your company practices and culture, the principles will ensure that you stay on top if you're already there. If you're not there, they can help turn it all around for you and get you there. Somebody learned this lesson in Harley Davidson about a dozen years ago.

Must go now. Carruthers, my personal valet, is just laying out my business lunch, nineties style: Velveeta "Cheese and Kav-ee-R" dip with a couple of crackers, washed down with a small glass of Snapple.

3

On Reinventing Your Product

John, Paul, George, Ringo . . . and who?

It is difficult to say exactly when I fell out with Paul McCartney. In the early sixties in Liverpool, we were great friends, close enough for him to offer me a place in his new band, the Beatles. I think he wanted me to head the woodwind section, but it doesn't matter now; I couldn't make it work for my schedule, and we gradually drifted apart.

I think it was our respective diets that caused the final, acrimonious parting. As I led my superstar life, jetting from banquet to banquet, I found I had to impose strict dietary rules to retain my awesome 28-inch waist, notably:

- If I couldn't lift it, I didn't eat it.
- If it didn't have lungs, I didn't eat it.
- If it had any green color in it, I didn't eat it.
- If anyone said, "It really tastes like chicken," (particularly in South Korea), I didn't eat it.
- If anything moved on the plate, I didn't eat it.

McCartney, of course, led by his Soya-friendly wife, Linda, went in an entirely different dietary direction, dedicating himself to rigid vegetarianism. His mission was accompanied by him whining and moaning at anybody who didn't see it his way—particularly somebody like me who's ingoing position to any debate on the subject is that tofu should be used to put out forest fires and that's all.

All this doesn't stop me from admiring the guy's work—and one aspect of his career development that many businesses can learn from. The Beatles had an astonishing decade of success, one probably unprecedented and probably not equaled since. Then *whammo!* It was all over, and four guys faced the future knowing that the status quo was irrevocably changed. What happened next has many parallels for business.

Ringo's approach was simple: to remain famous because he was famous, and it is an astonishing tribute to the Beatles' heritage that he still manages to pick up a few inches in the gossip columns and frothy magazines. McCartney, of course, chose a different approach, seeing the Beatles as a start, not a finish; and as a means, not an end. Constantly trying new things, risking critical derision and the erosion of the glow of Beatlemania, he is arguably more successful than ever some 25 summers later, filling stadiums around the world at an unprecedented level.

Like the Beatles, a business will often—often predict-
ably—come to the end of a golden period, because of self-
inflicted wounds, adverse
market forces, or both.
Cycles happen. The business
then faces the challenge of
continued growth in a whole
new world (like McCartney),
or *drifting in a memory* of the
old (as Ringo did). It is all
about *self-reinvention*, the
constant challenge to put
yourself in front of the cus-
tomer in new, attractive guises. There are a number of
ways you can go about it:

> **S**elf-reinvention:
> **the constant**
> **challenge to put**
> **yourself in front of**
> **the customer in**
> **new, attractive**
> **guises.**

- Simply keep upgrading your core product, like
  Microsoft Windows.

- Get there through innovation, like Sony, which does
  not sell a product today that was invented more
  than 20 years ago.

- Keep an edge through technology, like Gillette or
  Intel.

- Toyota and Nissan wanted to grow by entering the
  luxury car market, but were unsure of the appropri-
  ateness of their brand names. They evolved Lexus
  and Infiniti to fill the bill. There's self-reinvention for
  you.

- Worship the god of quality and you can keep your
  golden period going . . . and going . . . and going.
  See Harley Davidson, Motorola, and Marks and
  Spencer (the UK retailer).

- When you can't (daren't?) change your product—like
  Coca Cola—make sure your marketing convinces
  your customers that the brand, although unchanged,
  is still relevant to their changing lives.

- Sometimes just plain old aggression works, as it seems to be doing for Rupert Murdoch and his communications conglomerate (notably Fox).
- Maybe you just go for add-ons—like CNN, then CNN Headline News, then CNN International. Burger King and McDonalds are now more than 40 years old. When their cycles went south for a while, they regained impetus (and growth) by adding drive thrus, then breakfast, then chicken and fish sandwiches.

Constant, constant self-challenge and reinvention have to happen. Not everything works; McCartney "crossed over" and cowrote a classical Oratorio that flew like an ostrich. Mistakes will be made, but remember that mistakes are not failures. Strangely enough, mistakes often help *avoid* failures.

There are many examples of corporate Ringos about, from the Swiss watch industry (with the notable exception of Swatch) to the mighty IBM, whose recent successes have been reduced to high fiving when Intel burps. But who cares?

I must go now. I have a call waiting, and I understand it's George Harrison. Apparently he's pissed about something . . .

4

On International Trading

Keep the body bags handy

I made a major miscalculation. The event was the Summit of the Americas, with more than 30 heads of state from the two continents assembled in Miami, and I had (natch) invited them to my south Florida pad for an intimate *soiree*. The miscalculation came in underestimating the accompanying entourage of spin doctors, hangers on, and quasi security agents, who totaled nearly 2,000 people and sorely tested the space and hospitality of my humble *chateau*.

A fine time was had by all, especially because I chose a cuisine of the finest English dishes, which went down very well after the interminable surfeit of *moros* they'd experienced over the last few days (although I did notice

Hillary looking very thoughtfully at a plate of beef tripe and mushy peas).

Because Bill and Hill were staying overnight, I opened up the East Wing and gave them full access to the Royal Suite—that's the one with a tasteful sign by the bed saying, "Princess Fergie slept here." Unfortunately, other guests of less pedigree have added some rather rude graffiti that has no place in a wholesome work such as this.

The whole deal got me thinking about internationalism and international trading. The advent of NAFTA, the ratification of the last round of GATT, the unification of Europe, and now the Summit of the Americas (with its commitment to eventual free trade based on the quaint concept of labor regulation amongst some of its members) is prompting a lot of companies to wake up to the idea of international trading. Of course, the real international traders had been at it long before these events (and they will prove to be the long-haul winners), but nonetheless, rallying to a cry of Better Late Than Never, many are now contemplating tentative cross-border steps.

The latecomers have woken up to the fact that it will be necessary to trade internationally to *defend* their business, not to mention seeking growth.

During the last half of my corporate life, I was involved in businesses that traded, by my calculation, in about 70 countries. I have probably spent more time in airport delays than most people spend in higher education. I have eaten things that my every fiber screamed at me to refuse. I have made every mistake in the book and today have scar tissue on scar tissue to prove it. Here are some thoughts to make your ride easier:

- Building your business internationally will be done on the backs of a few buccaneering people from your home-based business going "over there." These guys are euphemistically called "ex pats" and, although they earn big bucks, they invariably come home in body bags, with a huge loss of experience to the company, and a high deterrent factor to anybody else thinking of following. To achieve success in this kind of program, the home company needs to *mentor* these people and *plan ahead* realistically. It's obvious but never done.

- It is easy to assume that the home country has a monopoly of wisdom about everything from product specification and marketing through the human resource issues such as cultural diversity and equal opprtunity. You have some wisdom, but you surely do not have a monopoly, so tread carefully here guys. Respect local traditions, ways of doing business, and social values; then you can slowly find a mix that is sustainable for both you and your trading partners.

  My personal ruling here was simply to treat each country as a restaurant that insists that neckties be worn: I either wear one or go someplace else. I do not create a scene and try and change the place's values. If the price is just too high for you to enter a country (for example, you are required to do something illegal or unethical, or your potential partner's own agenda is just too divergent from yours), find another avenue.

- Develop local people as quickly as possible to run your outpost—particularly the chief executive. Depending on the size of the subsidiary, it is likely there will always be a mix of locals and ex pats, and I have found that Finance/Treasury is always a good bet for the home country player. In the long haul, however, properly supported locals are best in almost all other aspects of the business.

- Choose your partners carefully. Rarely can effective new-county entry be achieved without alliances— usually financial or for the production or distribution of your product. My rule was never to choose the first and obvious one, and to avoid the "brand collectors" who seek to add your name to the 700 western brands they already distribute. Find somebody who wants to grow with you.

- Last is what I call the CIA factor, which is perhaps the most important. CIA is simply my shorthand for "Confusion from Implied Assumptions" and reflects the ever present communication snafus that prevail in modern business but that are heightened by geographic and language gaps. I have not yet seen a microchip portable translator that includes the phrase *I thought you meant*, but they ought to; it's probably the most frequently used international business phrase. To avoid it you need patience, empathy, and communication overkill—none of which you normally carry by the bucketful.

> *I thought you meant:* **The most frequently used international business phrase.**

The differences in nations remain truly astonishing. If the Summit of the Americas wasn't enough, I was reminded of it again recently when an old pal from England visited, and we walked the length of an enormous local shopping mall one rainy day. He then paused for lunch: *three liters of draft beer.* This struck me as a real "guys" sort of lunch, English style.

Of course, I have been in the U.S. for six years now, and my lunch consisted of whining to get a salt-free, fat-free pretzel accompanied by a (small) glass of designer bottled water.

5

More on Brands

He needs this putt to stay 15 under par . . .

Poor, poor old Gary Player.

Distraught by the loss of NFL football ("That's not all that important to us") and some important affiliates ("Have we?"), CBS went for broke in the sports ratings recently by filming the "These Really Are the True Legends of Golf $200 Million Skins Game." It will be televised later in the year.

Trevino, Palmer, Nicklaus, and Player were invited, but poor Gary fell victim to the flu. Understandably, I was asked to make up the four, which is how I came to be walking down the fifth fairway with three of the world's biggest brands.

Yep. That's what I said: brands.

Lee, Arnie, and Jack were fascinated by this thought process and, as we walked up to the fifth green after three of us had played up, you could have heard a tee drop as I held court. (Nicklaus had already picked up. Wild drive. Out of bounds, left. Again!)

"Branding is a *fundamental* of wealth creation and capitalism," I informed them, using my my throaty, intellectual voice, "and is probably the genuine oldest profession. You have a product of distinction and consistency, you identify people who you think will want to buy your product, you convey a message about your product's distinction and consistency to those people (we call this *marketing*), and then you sell it at a high margin. Part of that margin goes into making your product even more distinct and consistent (we call this *product development*). Part of it goes into telling *more* people more about your product's distinction and consistency, and part goes in bucketfuls to your stockholders."

> **B**randing is a fundamental of wealth creation.

There was no stopping me: "Done properly, the thing spirals upward and looks unstoppable. A nasty side effect, however, can threaten the success. Your firm gets bloated and inefficient, cost control gets sloppy, and the chairman starts playing with the marketing budget, sponsoring things like Golf Tournaments."

The last comment caused much hilarity on the green, and Arnie missed his long birdie putt. Lee and I looked at each other a little nervously because nobody had won a skin yet, and there was now $72 million riding on this hole.

I carried on, all calmness on the surface, "Many people, who should know better, think brands died on Marlboro Friday in 1992, when Philip Morris, having followed the formula for years, suddenly dropped its price in an attempt to stop losing market share to unbranded cigarettes. The effect of this move was impressive. I do not know what the opposite of an orgasm is, but the stock market immediately had one."

Lee burst out laughing and gunned his putt 10 feet past the hole.

I was on my own now, but I couldn't waste the chance of an audience like this. "Brands are far, far from dead," I went on, dramatically waving my Kmart putter to emphasize the point, "but a new challenge has been added. Consumers have come out of this last recession scarred, cynical, and uncertain. They still want products of distinction and consistency, and purchasers will pay for them—but not to a point that funds a company's inefficiency and the chairman's Hobby Farm. And *somehow consumers know what this is.*

"We must now add a third 'must have' to a brand's properties, and that is *value;* and we must cut the crap about perceived value and start talking about real, touchable, feelable value. The new challenge is to make sure brands are stripped of all support costs other than those essential to deliver a 9 out of 10 rating on all three properties. And remember, *everything* is a brand—a school, a credit card, a phone service. Everything. Not just a soap powder."

I bent over my putt and sent the ball on its way.

The greens were slow, and the ball was still running as I looked up and finished my seminal thesis. "A totally new approach is needed. A golf analogy is appropriate, because many associated with brands approach them as golfers whose lives, understandably, revolve around the current week's tournament. They find that they occasionally win one, finish well a few times, finish badly usually a few more times, and sometimes miss the cut.

"Those who understand brands, however, approach them like golfers who, while recognizing that this week's tournament and earnings are important, know that what counts in the end is performance on the *tour*, not the tournament. Ups and downs will happen, but over time, if your performance provides distinction, consistency, and value to a degree that merits it, you are deemed as one of the Greats."

Their eyes followed my ball, but their ears strained to catch every word. I smiled at the three of them, and went on in a dramatic whisper, "Amazingly, when the world—or the customer, as we call it—does define a Great, it is rarely based just on earnings but rather on how the Great earned his winnings, including things like style and personality. And so shall it be with brands."

The silence was broken as my ball rattled the cup and dropped in. Seventy-two million dollars! Enough for dinner for four on Miami Beach, *and some change.*

The Rise and Fall of "Ho-Hum"

And a very rude word that goes in the middle

Arriving back in the U.S., I was greeted at the airport by hordes of press who wanted to know my first response to the news that Phil Gramm had declared that he would stand for the presidential nomination in 1996. I told them that my first reaction was to wonder if the Christmas cards he had been sending me would ever be worth as much as those I received from Gandhi, Kurt Cobain, Yuri Gagarin, and His Holiness Pope John Paul the Bestseller.

I do not joke about these things: Much of my enormous wealth has come from these bits of personal memorabilia, and I have been offered big money for such as the signed

Little Red Book that Mao sent me on my twenty-first birthday. My prize, of course, is the old bra that Grace Kelly left on the back seat of my Jaguar in the fifties sometime. Surely someday that will make my children rich.

Anyway, back to Phil Gramm, the Texas senator untouched by charisma or good looks. My second response, which, of course, I do not give the press, is to repeatedly mutter the letters *HFH* to myself.

This joined my personal collection of acronyms early in my time at Burger King, when I decided to bring the worldwide management team together to boldly see whether we had any idea why we'd been peeing on our own shoes for about 10 years. I brought in one of the world's great business gurus (at a cost which was roughly the equivalent of Greece's GNP) to help us in the quest, and I remember us both standing in the semidark at the side of the stage, me nervously, as we waited for the cue for me to go on and announce him.

I could hear him talking to me, but only about one in three words was sinking in. Suddenly, with awful clarity, he was telling me that, to make sure he had all his facts, he had visited a Burger King the previous evening. I froze in absolute horror. That was all I needed: details of some nightmare experience in front of 400 folks I was trying to lift. But he went on quickly to say that everything had been fine. The place was clean; the service quick; the food hot, good, and cheap; and my heart started beating again. Phew! I turned to go on, and then heard him whisper gently, as if to himself: "HFH." Well, he didn't actually use the letters, he said the words—the first one being *ho*, the last one being *hum*, and the middle one you can go figure.

In its own way, it was worse than relating a nightmare experience. What he was saying was that *when we did it right* it was still pretty ordinary. Damned by faint praise.

HFH has stuck with me ever since, simply because the world is full of it. Look around and see things and people that are OK but nothing special. They do a job but leave no ripples in the water, and now Gramm seeks the presidency after Bush and Clinton, surely two of the most HFH leaders in U.S. history. The planet is swimming in a sea of HFH world leadership.

HFH products and services—particularly the latter—abound. Yet it is in the service area that the real opportunity exists to rise above the clutter and imprint yourself on the customer's memory as something special warranting a repeat purchase.

> It is in the service area that the real opportunity exists to rise above the clutter.

A couple of years ago, I went to the Caribbean for a holiday, booked at short notice with a major hotel chain. In the bedroom was a sign on the dresser saying, "Please look under the bed." It intrigued me, so I did. I saw another handwritten sign saying, "Yes, I clean under here as well. Rosie." Wonderful, wonderful, wonderful. No HFH here, but a strange thing did happen: I forgot the resort's brand name (despite the millions of dollars spent on advertising) and I remember it as Rosie's Place and recommend it frequently.

At one time I was responsible for about 2,000 bars in England, and we figured it would help us beat the HFH factor if we got our bar staff to learn customers' first names. So we had a competition to see how many names one person could remember, assuming that someone knowing 25, maybe 50, would clean up the prizes. The winner reeled off 400, and then we found out that the bar she worked was (surprise, surprise) wonderfully successful.

The key to both these crazy—but true—examples is first to recognize the need to rise above HFH, then to mobilize your people to do so. In the price/product/service cocktail that you offer your customers, service is the magic wand to rising above HFH—just as it is the way you fall below it if you get it wrong. Between 70 percent and 90 percent of decisions made not to repeat a purchase are based on poor *service*, not *product* or *price*.

A Burger King franchise once missed a sandwich from a drive-thru order (no, really?), and a frustrated customer telephoned in to complain. The restaurant manager then got the sandwich delivered to the customer's office within 10 minutes, which makes a nice customer service story, if a little on the HFH side.

What made it different was a knock on the customer's door at lunchtime the next day, with the restaurant manager there saying, "Sorry about yesterday. Have lunch on us today."

What happened next was strange. In the customer's own words he said that he and his family talked about it over dinner that night—something they'd never normally have done if the meal had been delivered properly in the first place. It was also something that all the millions Burger King spends on advertising had never got that family doing. And yet they were fans of Burger King and ate there a lot.

What we've got here is a couple of simple, cheap acts of common sense and courtesy, conducted by a restaurant manager who had been enabled and encouraged to think and act that way which then made all the difference. He took a mistake, went straight through HFH without pausing, and turned it into a jewel of word-of-mouth marketing.

Ever vigilant in my research, as a frequent traveler across the Atlantic, I've been looking for an equivalent to HFH I can use in Europe.

At last I think I have it; I think I have it: EuroDisney (motto: *Service sans Sourire*).

7

On Advertising

And please wipe your upper lip

I had a routine doctor's appointment this morning. At first glance, everything seemed to be in the right place, properly attached and ticking nicely, but the detailed scan suddenly threw up one worrying variance. Since March of this year, I have put on 172 pounds, and my cholesterol level has shot up to an unusual (the doctor says) level of 975.

At last we trace the cause. Apparently, the only thing I have been doing differently has been the consumption, on average, of 1,318 glasses of milk each day since March. On reflection, there seems no doubt that I have been influenced by the magnificent marketing campaign for that fine product, as illustrated by a selection of the world's celebrated hard bodies sporting a moist white mustache and hitting us wannabes right between the eyes.

What great advertising this is, knocking Nike of its long-held pedestal position with me. (I also have 2,499 pairs of sneakers.)

Effective and efficient (both are important) advertising is now an endangered species. Time was, not so long ago, when you could put your brand in the hands of an appropriate agency, spend an aggressive—but not surreal—amount of cash on TV time, and sit back and enjoy guaranteed sales and market share growth. Oh, those were the days.

Three things have changed that forever:

- The increase in clutter and competition in the marketplace. Brand proliferation is now epidemic, with every sector containing a range of big players at each others' throats. And these players often confuse the customer. Advertising gurus add to the mayhem by inventing sectors where none exist, as in the super-duper-super-super-SUPER ice cream category. Gimme a break, guys. *It's ice cream.*

- Ninety percent of TVs now have a remote control and a wide (and growing) range of channels. There is no need to sit through a commercial break, so there can be no more captive audience for advertising. The "zap factor" (as the marketeers have christened it) is now a major inhibitor to reaching target audiences without spending crazy amounts of money.

- The number of media vehicles has exploded. Apart from the obvious TV channel–range growth, radio, magazines, local newspapers, sponsorships, billboards, retail merchandising spots, catalogs, the Internet, and multimedia are just some of the choices facing the head of advertising as he or she tries to figure out the best way to hit the right target market with the most impact for the least cash. Good luck.

The effect of these changes is that we have all become nearly blind to the advertised message. In the best book I ever read on the subject (*Guts—Advertising from the Inside Out*, published by Amacom, 1989), John Lyons estimates that the average American, on an average day, is exposed to about 1,800 advertising messages—from the minute the radio goes on in the morning to the time the TV is switched off at night.

Let's just work with that number and play a game. You (yes, you!) were exposed to that number yesterday. OK, now name *one*. See? Nearly blind.

So how do you beat that challenge as an advertiser? To some extent you can do it with dollars, either by saturation bombing all media with your message so that everybody sees it and hears it again and again until *something* just has to stick. Or you can do it by taking spots in major televised events (such as the Super Bowl) at millions of dollars a pop. McDonald's does either or both as well as any, simply because the corporation spends more than most.

The only other way is through genius—creative genius. There is no known formula for this, which is why creative geniuses make lumps of cash, wear heavy boots in the office, and doff weird spectacles.

> Take the distinction of your product and reach your target market with it in a way that is truly memorable.

The basic rules are to take the distinction of your product and reach your target market with it in a way that is truly *memorable*. But that's like saying to aspiring artists that they must use paint and a brush—out of a million attempts the vast, vast, majority would be crap and some would be OK. And one would be truly memorable.

I wish you well with your search for the Holy Grail; one real success can make a career. But a final word of warning: You've got to take risks. All mass markets are made up of individuals and, today, they have attitudes. These are not stifled anymore; they influence behavior. What will make an ad memorable and irresistible to some will almost certainly upset others. No, you don't have to take it to the lengths of Benetton, but the opposite extreme—advertising designed so that it absolutely cannot possibly upset anybody—is doomed to fail.

Back to my milk. It's wonderful for my midlife crisis, which has just celebrated its fifth anniversary. I dread its ending. Hollywood has got wind of it, and we believe there's now enough material for three screenplays with the provisional titles of: *Midlife Crisis (1), Midlife Crisis (The Sequel),* and *Midlife Crisis with a Vengeance.* Bruce Willis has been approached.

2

Power to the People

Yeah, right

Introduction

"Let's just try that bit again. I think it might come over as more sincere if you paused before you came out with the key words. Maybe you could raise your arms a bit?"

Zoie Peterson was head of the company's PR team. Her voice drifted out of the dark, otherwise empty, auditorium. The lone figure on the platform, partially hidden by the speaker's lectern, grimaced his annoyance and reshuffled his script.

Jim Francisco was the CEO, and tomorrow was a big day. The empty seats would be full of managers brought together for the annual convention.

Nothing betrayed his frustration at this whole rehearsal process except a couple of tiny beads of sweat glistening in the front roots of his immaculately styled hair.

"OK, Zoie. How does this sound?"

He paused. Carefully, he raised his arms into a position of semi-supplication. The front of his french cuffs protruded evenly from the sleeves of his dark European suit. He raised his voice.

"People. People. People. Make no mistake. Our people are our greatest asset."

The words echoed across the ghostly auditorium before the magic of the moment was crushed by Zoie's shrill voice ringing out, "Wonderful. Just wonderful. You'll have them in the palm of your hand."

The young captain of industry grunted something that sounded self-satisfied and gathered up his papers. Waving dismissively, he headed for the stage side door, muttering to himself.

Unfortunately, he had forgotten to unhook his portable microphone and the constant repetition of the words "People are our greatest asset" was picked up quite clearly by Zoie and a rather surprised sound engineer.

Also picked up were his final words as he left the stage: "People are our greatest asset. I just wish we could pay 'em less. And boy do I wish we had a lot fewer of the fuckers."

The preceding is not an extract from anything. I confess I made it up. It is entirely fictional in detail. The principles, however, echo around most boardrooms every day.

The great business paradox is this: We live in a time when organizations are smaller, flatter, and tighter. More pressure is put on fewer folks. There is more competitive edge attributed to intellectual capital and people skills than ever before. It is a time when people should be recognized as treasures and treasured. But they are not.

Instead, work forces are alienated and cynical. Loyalty exists only to a mentor or a team, not to the organization. "Us" and "Them" are alive and well.

Leaders are thought to be self-centered manipulators, liars not to be trusted who are driven by short-termism and paranoia. This is fair. Most will score four out of five.

> **I**t is a time when people should be recognized as treasures and treasured. But they are not.

A big part of the cause, of course, lies with the accountants—those anal retentives who are inexorably taking over the governance of the planet.

The world sees people as assets. The accountants say, "Nah!"

They say people are *expenses.* If you invest in hiring a person, he or she is an expense of the business, not an asset. If you train and develop that person, it is not an investment in the same way as adding onto a building. It is an additional expense, like the use of more electricity.

Expenses have three main properties:

- They are a pain in the ass to the short-term earnings of the business and therefore to the earnings per share and earnings multiples.
- By definition, expenses are usually discretionary. It may cost you in the short term, but you can usually stop any expense.
- If you suddenly avoid a whole chunk of expenses, the business looks a lot better. To some eyes.

Now the accountants pull off their master trick. You are allowed to take a one-off "restructuring charge" whereby you can get rid of a humongous chunk of expenses (i.e., people), and disguise the cost of so doing as you then account for the benefits to the admiring world.

Leaders, of course, know all of this by heart. So do the people. So everybody knows that employment has become a science of sufferance; if the organization can possibly do without you, it surely will.

It comes as no surprise that the work ethic and loyalty of the work force has been holed below the water line. Most employees would much rather be doing something else. Working your ass off doing twice as much as a previous generation, under three times the pressure for (maybe) 5 percent more money—all the while waiting for the dawn raid that sees you out of a job—is nobody's idea of a ball.

Against that background, it is tough to talk about enlightened people management. A marriage where both parties would rather be someplace else can survive, and the parties may even prosper. But it needs another name. It is an arrangement, an *existence.*

As ever, people are resilient. What else would you expect of a species that produced Keith Richard? It's just that some exist better than others.

Somehow, some organizations and some groups of folk get the poison out of the air in the greenhouse, and people grow and flourish.

Humankind has spent centuries studying diseases in the hope of finding appropriate remedies. We have not spent much time searching for forces that can infect a body with health and spread it like a positive plague. We have no word for the opposite of *virus.*

But some organizations have found something along those lines. Some have generated ideas, practices, and policies that enable everyone to prosper individually, and for the organization to achieve more than the sum of its parts—and beat the hell out of its competition.

This section's essays are grains of sand in a desert of writing about power and empowerment. But this stuff can work. I have been there, seen it, and damn near bought the T-shirt.

When it does work, it is a beautiful thing.

8

On the Fear of Fear

You thought the marathon was a road race

We drove for about an hour out of Athens to the north and then stopped the car. We were high above the olive line, and way, way below us the sunlight danced on the Bay of Marathon.

There was a long period of reflective silence. When we started to talk, the subject was naturally corporate reengineering.

My young companion, one of 40 or so full-time research assistants I employ in my studies to find ways for a kinder, more rewarding business world, could barely contain his enthusiasm for the idea: "Reengineering will—it *must*—provide the remedy for the ills of Western business," he half shouted in his intensity. "Every company I know is doing it. It has to be the cornerstone for a new tomorrow."

"I fear not, Michaelis," I replied in that calm, measured voice I do so well, "and I fear not for two reasons."

My words seem to hang in the cool, air conditioned elegance of the Porsche. I continued: "The first reason is that the concept itself is simply being abused. Done *properly*—that is, completely restructuring the firm around its seminal processes—it is truly a means to the ultimate management goal of doing more, better, with less. Unfortunately, in the vast majority of cases, it is being applied as a title to simple, guttural, downsizing—the science of doing less, worse, with less."

> **S**imple guttural downsizing: the science of doing less, worse, with less.

Michaelis was silent for a while, sprawled in his seat. Accepted as one of the finest young minds to come out of the Nana Mouskouri School for Advanced Management Studies in Athens, I could see that he was nonetheless drifting into that unnecessarily defensive posture that most New Age thinkers signal when challenged. Well, my sons do, anyway.

"So, what's the second reason?" he muttered. A little belligerently, I thought.

I told him that it was much more subtle than the first. Reengineering was, in fact, just another (the latest) mechanistic "strategy tool" available to management, just as centralization (then decentralization) had been. Just as matrix management, total quality management, the pursuit of excellence, liberation management, and entrepreneurship had, in turn, been the answers. But not one of them *fully* did the job, because there had been a Missing Link.

I told him how I had searched for the Missing Link, and found it in the strangest place—an interview in the

London Times with Ronnie Lott, the legendary San Francisco 49ers' football player. He had explained that if you pulled out of a tackle at the last minute, not only did you lose effectiveness but there was also a good chance you could hurt yourself. To be really effective you had to *block out the gods of fear.*

"And that is why it will be no more successful than anything else," I continued. "Western business is riddled with fear, in every aspect of everything it undertakes.

> It is right we should fear failure, but in the workplace we are now frightened to make mistakes.

And I am not just talking about the fear of losing your job, ever present though that is today. I'm talking about why some great American brands aren't world leaders. Why there is paranoia about the EEC, GATT, and NAFTA. Why there is never a truly honest personal performance appraisal in business. It is right that we should fear failure, but in the workplace we are now frightened to make mistakes. The two have become confused, and the consequences are horrendous.

"It is why new products are market tested to death—or worse, to blandness. It is why powerful corporate Public Relations departments disseminate selected truths, Goebbels-like, to vigilante stockholders, challenging analysts, inquiring regulators, and increasingly alienated employees. *Everything is inhibited by fear.* Reengineering will prove no more of a panacea for all capitalism's problems than any other doctrine because it will be planned behind closed doors, communicated with dishonesty, and executed with inhibitions."

There was a long silence before my companion responded. His voice seemed strained. "Is it even possible to block out the gods of fear?"

"Just look down there," I pointed to the distant bay. "Nearly 2,500 years ago the terrifying combined armies of the Medes and Persians swept through the Eastern Mediterranean and landed there, with Athens the next target. They were faced by a heavily outnumbered Greek army, with five of their generals voting to retreat at speed (thus inventing the Boston Marathon). The other five generals voted to defend their ground to the death. The decision was left to their leader, Miltiades, who opted for neither. He chose to attack the enemy on the run, routed them, and rewrote the history of civilization."

The effect of this on Michaelis was astonishing. He was frozen in his seat, his face white with disbelief. "You know, don't you?" he whispered. "But how *could* you know? That I am the seventieth generation of Miltiades?"

My reply was gentle but assured (another one I do well). "I know *everything*. My researches and researchers miss nothing. I know you are the fruit of the loins of the man who truly blocked out the gods of fear. You see, reengineering does not even begin to provide the answer; that answer truly lies with the courage of your ancestor, a courage that must be applied when you use the strategy tool of your choice. In him, through you and people like you, we must find the Spirit of the New Capitalism—a spirit that does not just shape our leaders but everyone."

I smiled enigmatically at the confused young man. At least, I think I did. Well, I tried to. It's not easy if you're not sure what it means.

On Empowerment

And the parable of the condoms

The fourth of the known five genders that promenade the sidewalks on Miami South Beach late on a Sunday morning walked by and was duly noted by my brunch companion, Eric Clapton. My thoughts were elsewhere.

"The new spirit of capitalism must recognize that success will come through people who are winners," I said to no one in particular. "But therein lies the paradox. The time when we most need capable and motivated people will be the time when we will have most alienated the workforce. Workers will be cynical, mistrusting, and resentful. Loyalty, if it exists at all, will be to a contract, a mentor, maybe a team, possibly a project. But not to the company." The words were far-reaching, and they hung in the late morning air.

My old pal Eric, who was with us for the weekend, looked across the table at me, his long legendary, calloused fingers picking at his bagel. He was quietly singing to himself in the new voice he developed for the *Unplugged* album. It was almost as though he was ignoring me.

I carried on, regardless, slipping into my own hip, rock star voice. "Them CEOs man, they're startin' to piss me off, man, talkin' like they do about people being the company's biggest asset, at the same time wiping out another herd like they were buffalo. What a bummer, man." I got the distinct feeling that my accent wasn't impressing him. Maybe a little too John Denver. Far out. Anyway, for whatever reason, the Great One resumed his search to spot the elusive fifth gender, squinting through his new Armani sunglasses.

My mind wandered back a few hours. I'd completed the first phase of my research of my study into empowerment. I now had more than a hundred of the best young business minds in the world, from the finest business schools, all diligently researching the task. All of them were thoughtful. The majority were women. We needed a new approach.

Only the previous day, I had concluded an exhaustive research session with Monique, an elfin, bright young thing from Academie EuroDisney, one of the excellent new schools emerging in the north of France. Her findings were depressing. "I've been reading *The Guinness Book of World Records*," she reported crisply and efficiently (and, frankly, in a very un-French like way), "and empowerment is now officially recognized as the biggest single gap between 'walk' and 'talk' in Western business."

I explained to her how this came to be: It is not *natural* for we Captains of Industry to empower people. I bravely gave her an example from my own casebook (nothing to do with industry, really, but one that illustrates the point vividly).

I had decided to give my eldest son a chunk of money, partly because it was his twenty-first birthday, but more importantly because I had been deeply influenced by the Menendez brothers' trial. I gave him the cash, then promptly tried to over-manage the process with rules for spending it and proposals for sensible invest-ments. Why did I do this? As one who had preached about empowerment, what stopped me from just letting him get on with it? From making his own mistakes? Finding his own solutions? Was it mistrust? A need to protect him? A need to protect me? Just *what* was I frightened of?

> **E**mpowerment is now officially recognized as the biggest single gap between "walk" and "talk" in Western business.

I came back to the present. By now, Eric was snoring gently. I carried on with my thoughts, this time aloud. "There is no doubt that empowerment is the key to the new spirit. I saw it so clearly after the hurricane. . ."

It was as if I had knifed him. He sat bolt upright, and I suddenly caught a glimpse of the old, ugly Clapton of twenty years ago. It was as if he was actually *bored* by my stories of Hurricane Andrew. I had to buy another caffe latte to restrain him.

I told him of the bizarre circumstances after the hurri-cane hit south Florida. How there were no buildings, no communications, no businesses, few basics. How I was chief executive of a business that had its world headquar-ters thoughtfully in the eye of the bloody thing. How a few people—employees, spouses, kids—did what they could in the first few days. How some took a pile of dol-lar bills and drove north till they found places they could buy basics, food, water, medical supplies, and so on, to bring back to distribute to our people.

I told him how one spouse came back from such a trip with condoms in the midst of the supplies. How no one questioned her, but that she saw raised eyebrows, and simply said: "Think."

Oh, how we thought then, that what people would want most during this time would be the comfort of their loved ones and that what they would need least would be an unwanted pregnancy. And how we marvelled at this woman's contribution, and wondered why we couldn't run our ordinary business like that. *With all our people using their minds fully to help the company through other (albeit less dramatic) changes and challenges.*

Eric remained silent as I spoke softly, the John Denver accent long gone, superceded by a gripping Anthony Hopkins–type tone. "It was astonishing. Truly. And *The Parable of the Condoms* has the key to this whole empowerment thing. Only the losers will not involve and empower people in future. The enlightened will involve their people in providing answers. But the winners will be firms who create, men-

> **The real winners will be the firms who create, mentally, the effects of a hurricane and start with nothing.**

tally, *the effects of a hurricane and start with nothing.* Who then involve their people in using their minds to help define *the questions* the business must ask about itself. And who then empower those people to shape and deliver the answers."

I think some of that went over his head, and I confess I spoke without the authority that can only come from total understanding of what you're talking about.

I took his silence to mean he was pondering the subject to see if there was a potential lyric in it. Then he let out a "whoop." He'd spotted his elusive target. The missing fifth gender. We could go now.

On Training and Motivation

And the secrets behind the aging of your CD rims

I often stare at my compact discs as they revolve, safe in the knowledge that the center is aging faster than the rim with every turn. It was, of course, Einstein who figured that out, during a lifetime in which he joined light to time, time to space, energy to matter, matter to space, and space to gravitation.

At the end of his life, when I knew him best, he was still trying to figure out a unity between gravitation and the forces of electricity and magnetism. That's how I remember him, in the Senate House in Cambridge, in an old sweater and carpet slippers with no socks, as we worked on the problems together in the early 1950s.

I was a child prodigy, wise beyond my years, and I would argue with him that he was a philosopher, not a mathematician. He would just smile. What was much more important to him was that I took his "beacon"—the General Theory of Relativity ($E = MC^2$)—and carried it forward.

> E = MC², or Effectiveness is created by Motivation and Capability.

That I did so is now part of history. I took it into a new dimension as a fundamental of business today: $E = MC^2$, or Effectiveness is created by Motivation and Capability. That's not motivation or capability, but both. Squared.

It's obvious, just like the old centers of your CDs. But it's so rarely delivered in modern business.

Simply translated, the equation means that however motivated you are (whether by threat or reward), there are some things you can't do unless you are trained and capable (like flying a plane, translating from Arabic, or tying your shoes . . .). Conversely, however well trained you are, nothing effective happens unless you are motivated—as many professional, highly gratified journalists will tell you: they do their best work when backed right up against a deadline.

Getting the formula right is a major challenge for business, and both the motivation and capability elements need careful thought.

Training (or making people capable) is a joke in Western business. It is estimated that less than 1.5 percent of revenue is reinvested in training, and that itself gets cut if revenues fall short because it is treated as an expense and not an investment for the company. On top of that, as functional illiteracy grows among Western adults, so does the complexity of most jobs, often bound up with high technology and computer applications. The biggest laugh of all is that training is still a "supply-side" science, inasmuch as individual training needs are still defined by the company, which then provides the time, plans, courses, and resources to meet those needs.

What a crock.

Every individual's training needs are different, however much jobs are alike—everybody has a different experience and/or skill level. It is the individual's prime responsibility—not the corporation's—to define and drive his or her own personal development.

Each year, staff should take time to think through their own *central* training needs (those required to do the existing job better), their *peripheral* training needs (those required to prepare for personal growth), and, finally, their *discretionary* needs (those skills not obviously needed but which an employee would like to have). At that stage the company gets into a conversation with the employee—listening and supporting, and challenging where appropriate. An agreed-upon personal development plan is then drawn up and resources identified to deliver it.

Follow these guidelines and the five loaves and five fishes that make up most training budgets can be used to the best possible effect, because the trainee now feels ownership. Training is relevant and adds personal value; it's not some dumb idea from the head office.

In the same way, classical thinking on motivation is just as daft and ineffective. Years ago, two smug snake-oil salesmen—Maslow (with his hierarchy of needs) and Herzberg (with his hygiene factors)—advanced theories that people soon satisfied their needs for money and from then on were motivated by more intangible rewards such as job satisfaction and recognition.

These approaches are also a crock. And they are still, incredibly, being taught at business schools in the 1990s. People do want both intangible and tangible rewards, but not sequentially—they want 'em together. But if you want real motivation, something that gets above and beyond performance, just stick with cash, particularly a chunk of cash in these times when penal personal tax rates make it hard to accumulate capital on a salary. If you want to double real motivation, tie the chunk of money reward to success in the business—particularly the *over*achievement of goals.

I was suffering from Maslow Myopia when I bought a small chain of restaurants in Switzerland in the mid-eighties. The chain was very successful, and as part of the due diligence process the owner told me how he motivated his restaurant staff, an approach that in his eyes was perhaps the biggest factor in their success. He simply paid the whole restaurant team the legal minimum Swiss wage each month or 20 percent of the sales income, whichever was the highest.

This had two astonishing effects. First, the team didn't want any additional staff hired so their *productivity* was tremendous. Second, *service* was marvelous because the team hated to lose customers because of the lost revenue directly to them. Not only that, they tried to sell extra desserts and drinks, and tried to get the customers to agree to come back soon. Herzberg would implode, but here you have one simple idea: motivating people to higher productivity, better service, and add-on and repeat sales. And the idea was purely based on money money money money . . .

$E = MC^2$. Like peaches and cream, motivation's no good without capability. Both are hard to achieve, but both suffer from overcomplication and overmanagement in business today. Get 'em both, and get 'em both simple.

All of this training insight stems from my deep friendship with Einstein when I was nine years old. You wouldn't believe what happened after I played soccer for Brazil when I was twelve. . .

11

On Working in Teams

Don't you spit on my blue polo shirt

Do I take on some dumb things or what? Pavarotti, my old drinking chum, was in Miami recently for his solo concert on the beach and popped 'round after the show to escape from Madonna and the gang.

Frankly, the *grappa* flowed a bit too freely. Before I knew it I had agreed to join him, José, and Placido for their (now to be called) Four Tenors concert in Rio later this year.

I'll be honest: I'm scared. I have a pleasing light tenor voice, but it's a bit rusty and I've been having difficulty recently, in the shower, with that high bit at the end of "Like a Bridge over Troubled Water." So how I'll get in shape for the soaring climax to *"Nessun Dorma"* (the advertising theme for the well known Japanese minivan) is beyond me.

And these guys will expect the best. When they perform together it has to be seamless. We're talking teamwork here.

Team, team, team. Everywhere it seems to be the word of the moment, particularly in business. If you landed from Mars, and you were daft enough to listen to how industry's heavy hitters told you how they ran their businesses, you'd come to the conclusion that the traditional organization was dead, that business was a fluid process of evolving and dissolving teams—big teams, little teams; strategic teams, tactical teams; all sorts of teams.

And you'd be so wrong.

Sure, teams play a part in business today, but overall, it's no more a part than they've played in the past. It's a bit like infidelity in the British royal family; it's been going on for centuries but, until now, nobody wrote or thought much about it. Suddenly it's a big deal.

Business has always been run by teams known under various guises: boards, groups, committees, subcommittees, task forces, councils, assemblies, or whatever. Strangely, because they've not been called "teams," lack of teamwork has been identified as part of the problem for business, not the solution, and simply giving the members of one of these some blue polo shirts with "Widget Development Team—Get Outta Our Way" on the front changes nothing unless it is accompanied by a complete paradigm shift in attitude.

Hegel, the gloomy German philosopher, despaired of anybody learning from history. But I've made enough mistakes in this particular science to light the way for all of you.

Following are a handful of natural laws that will enable you to deliver what everybody stupidly seems to think is automatic—that your team is more effective and efficient in task management than any of its predecessors.

- *Assembling* the team is obviously key, but heed a word of warning here. The world of sport has shown that there are two basic team models, the first being exemplified by a rowing crew where everybody weighs the same, shares the same height, and moves in absolute unison. The second is one, such as a soccer team, where you have real diversity—some big, some small; some faster, some slower; some highly skilled, some journeymen; some highly paid superstars, some lowly paid rookies. Away from the game field there are tensions and different agendas. They are notoriously hard to manage, but on game day they come together as a unit and win. However attractive the first model might appear to somebody assembling a team, leave it for the river. The second model is the one you want—but be prepared to be exhausted. Also be prepared to win.

- A word on *numbers.* At a major corporation I worked for, I looked forward with excitement* to the first meeting of a task team in which I was to be included. The boardroom had been booked for the meeting (which was the first bad sign), and when I got there, 22 people were crowded 'round the table, with backups sitting against the walls. We got nowhere, and I created my second law of teams: Hold up both your hands in front of you, fingers and thumbs spread. Count 'em. What you have

> Hold up both your hands in front of you, fingers and thumbs spread. Count 'em. What you have is exactly *twice* the maximum number you should have in any team.

---

*No I didn't. I lie.

is exactly *twice* the maximum number you should
have in any team. Effective teams need to debate
quickly (and objectively), make decisions fast, and
communicate constantly among themselves. Sure,
they will need to work with, work at, or represent
other people, but include more than five in the actual team? Forget it.

- When a team has gathered, it's important for it to *set
its own goals.* One school of thought is that a team
should define its objectives, then set measurable success criteria for each. In other words, how will the
team know it has completed
the task successfully? A
more radical approach
would be for the team to define, in advance, how they
would know if they'd failed
the mission, an approach
stemming from the school
that believes real delegation
is the delegated ability to
fail. I don't like either approach: I like a team to
agree, at the outset, *why, when, and how it will dis-
band.* Think about it.

> Team philosophy
> should be to seek
> *occasional
> forgiveness* rather
> than *constant
> permission.*

- I also like a team to be ballsy. Individuals in business tend to be intimidated by people or circumstances, but the collective responsibility and
accountability of a team can enable it to be bolder
than the sum of its parts, take a few more risks, and
cut a few more corners. The team philosophy should
be to seek *occasional forgiveness* rather than *constant
permission.*

- Last, but by no means least, do not meet every Monday at 10:30 A.M.—or on any other preset calendar
basis. Meet when the need arises and don't meet

unless there is a preagreed purpose. This puts a lot of responsibility on the leader, but there is nothing less effective (or more frustrating) than to meet at a preagreed time, without preparation, simply because "we needed to get some meeting times in the calendar."

Teams, teams, teams.

Do you know, I think I'm going to be OK. I will be ready for the gig in Rio. My voice will be fine provided I gargle regularly and can put on about 175 pounds before the event. So, away! Away! To Burger King! To Burger King!

On Women in Business

And the fruits of a single gardenia

I know many were suspicious of my relationship with Billie Holiday, and gossip columns often hinted we were lovers.

Absolutely not so. But it was true that we had a deep and lasting influence on each other while I was her manager during the late 1920s. It was I, for example, who first pinned a gardenia in her hair. It was in her dressing room at the Cotton Club in 1929 after a particular triumph, and that symbol of our friendship became a permanent part of her imagery.

Her influence on me was equally lasting, because it was from her that I learned much about women in business, and about discrimination and diversity—issues that have become hot buttons of sensitivity in business today.

The real lesson she taught me is that the discrimination issues concerning women in business and general diversity are entirely separate subjects, and that's something not learned by today's corporate elite who insist on lumping the two of them together under the suspicious nomenclature of Cultural Diversity. This is a science that becomes even more dubious when it becomes the subject of something called *workshops*.

Women in business is a subject with issues all of its own. Let's start with a series of questions; answer each with a simple yes or no:

- After World War II, when my parents married and I arrived, my mother gave up her career as an executive secretary and remained a full-time mother and homemaker until my younger sister and I left the nest. I don't think she thought she had many options. She was pretty smart, huh? (Yes/No)

- A generation later, my wife did the same. This time it really was an option, and the choice was only made after lots of thought and debate. Pretty dumb, huh? (Yes/No)

- A woman I know, working in the media business, had two children. She worked virtually right up to delivery and was back at work days afterward. She and her husband employed a full-time nanny and cheerfully balanced homemaking, parenthood, and full-time careers. Pretty smart, huh? (Yes/No)

- Another woman I know told me that, in a particularly stressful meeting with her boss, she cried. Pretty dumb, huh? (Yes/No)

- A male boss I know was concerned that a woman who worked for him was dressing too "sexily" (his definition) for his firm's image and that she risked upsetting some clients. He very carefully broached the subject with her, suggesting she "dress down." Pretty dumb, huh? (Yes/No)

- Another male boss, concerned that a female subordinate was dressed a little too casually (his definition) for the rather smart firm they both worked for, carefully suggested she dress up a little. I suspect he had Demi Moore in mind. Pretty smart, huh? (Yes/No)

- Here's a tricky one. A female boss was concerned that one of her employees, also a female, was disrupting morale by flexing her personal worktime and habits too much. There was no actual problem with the work being done (in fact it was excellent and on time), but she was felt to be unnecessarily disruptive. Pretty dumb, huh? (Yes/No)

That's it. Test over.

OK. I confess. I cheated. If you answered "yes" or "no" to *any* of those questions, you are a lost cause. Quit this essay now and go find something on TV. Anything.

The correct answer to these questions is that there *are* no correct answers at policy level. There cannot be a right rule for everybody and every circumstance in life or business, which is exactly why companies continue to burn their fingers trying to manage these sensitive issues.

Women are an extensive part of modern business. What's more they are in it on equal terms: Business needs them just as much as they need business. These terms paint a very different picture from the patronizing tokenism and cheap secondary labor supply scene of 30 years ago.

Fundamentals have changed:

- The price of play in today's materialistic society is higher. To many families, a second flow of income is a necessity.

- "Standard" family architecture has changed dramatically. Many women now head households. Birth rates are lower, the population is aging. Singles abound.

- The nature of work has undergone profound change. Just after the Second World War, 70% of jobs required physical skills. By the end of the nineties, 70% will require cerebral skills.

- Technology—in the form of practical, affordable, safe birth control—has made it a genuine option to delay or avoid parenthood. If you are given real choice and can make the decision freely, whatever you choose is right because it's *right for you.*

It's fair to say that business has responded sluggishly (at best) to these changed circumstances. Many mistakes have been made, but the fundamental one is deep set. It is the mistake of insisting that these issues be addressed at policy level, that business must have a set of well-meaning policies that respond to the issues of women sharing the workplace.

What this means, of course, is that women are treated as women, some mythical creatures full of unfathomable logic, strange vulnerabilities, and exotic no-go areas. It means that they are addressed as physically weaker, but I know physically strong women and woefully weak guys. It means they are addressed as mothers, but I know many single/childless women and some single-parent men. It means they are thought of as sensitive, but I know men who cry and women who don't.

And so on, and so on, ad nauseum.

When will business learn that it doesn't employ people? That people policies are dumb? When will it understand that it actually employs John and Janet, José and Consuela, Pierre and Francine? That the way to recruit, retain, and develop the best people for the best results is to build an employment contract, of infinite variety, around a personal relationship with the individual?

It can't be that difficult a lesson to grasp. We seem to be employing fewer people. We say they are our greatest asset. We already pay people differently and give them different cars or car allowances. Most of them have different delegated authorities. The existing distinctions are already extensive. It cannot be that hard to match the required flexibility of most modern jobs with the required flexibility of modern individuals, male or female. If somebody wants a different per diem allowance for travel because he or she is concerned about appearances and spends more on laundry and hairdressing, so what? Build it into the total deal.

Sure, if you're an airline pilot, you can't build much flexibility into your working times or location, but most people aren't airline pilots, and many jobs can be done today whenever and wherever you can plug in a fax, phone, and PC.

Treat everybody as individuals? Build employment contracts that way? No more "people" policies? Aaaggh! Those fine people who are in Human Resource departments will issue a Salman Rushdie–style Fatwah on me. It simply can't be done.

Yeah, it can be done. It must be done. It means managers will have to manage their people as individuals again, something they haven't done since HR was invented because it has been seen as too time consuming and deflective from the real management task.

This individualization becomes the *real* management task. It also means that everyone in the organization has a mentor, Japanese style, to provide checks and balances for the one-to-one relationship. This is a system that is largely ignored in the West, and it is stupid to do so. It works.

This approach does, of course, support the thesis that companies should only directly employ those people essential to their core competencies, and contract the rest out—quite simply following the maxim that if you are to relate to individuals effectively, don't try and do it to too many of them. But it doesn't require a lot of new skills, just a lot of new thinking.

Now the bad news.

I do not expect dynamic changes to the current uneasy peace for women employed in big corporations. Such corporations are hung up on muddled concepts of fairness and treating everybody in the same way when, in fact, that's the last thing the people want and the business needs.

I do see dramatic change, however, in the vibrant small service business sector, fueled by corporate contraction and flexible location technology. These are often run by individuals for individuals and provide individualized services for the big corporations. History may show this explosion in the growth of small businesses to be the missing link to eventually getting it right for women in business across the whole spectrum of industry.

Hey. A teaspoonful of common sense would also help this particular world go around easier. When I was a kid it was drilled into me that I should hold the door for a woman and not take my seat at the dining table until the women were seated, holding their chairs for them if necessary.

I'm not sure I could stop doing these actions today if I wanted to, and I don't. But they're not a piece of implicit "Me Tarzan, you pathetic Jane" symbolism, they're just things I learned as manners that make for a nicer world. Like a lot of such gestures, they can be misinterpreted— innocently or maliciously—and can be seen as part of the problem, not the solution. Maybe everybody could just lighten up a wee bit? Occasionally couldn't we all give the other side the benefit of the doubt? Maybe we'll even learn to enjoy each other's individuality and not feel threatened by it?

All this from an affectionately placed gardenia in a woman's hair.

And we haven't talked about cultural diversity yet. Be still, my beating heart.

13

On Cultural Diversity

Next time, God is contemplating a less ambitious project

Captains of industry, like me, actually enjoy long plane journeys. They get time to unwind and ponder some of life's unanswerable questions, such as:

- What on earth happened to the Elephant Man? I mean, he made a great movie six or seven years ago but hasn't done anything since. Strange.
- Is it possible Sting is more pretentious than Pink Floyd? (That's a toughie.)
- Who first put the words *cultural* and *diversity* together in one sentence? And was he or she shot? If not, why not?

As if the world hadn't enough stupid ideas already (nouvelle cuisine?), it seems there is a need to invent new concepts or words that add no value.

We had *continuing,* we now have *ongoing* (which is ever so helpful). We had something called an *open meritocracy* and we now have *cultural diversity.* And we have it big time.

A whole industry has now been spawned, and if a week goes by in business without a workshop, seminar, lecture, and a whole bunch of new thoughts authored on the subject, it is classed (officially) as barren.

This brave new world spawned something called *affirmative action,* which is fine provided it is handled like the Ebola virus out of Zaire—very, *very,* carefully.

I can already see some ruffled feathers out there, so let us pause and figure some things out together. The premise behind all this is as follows: Any group or organization will benefit if the people in it are multidimensional and contribute openly to their full potential. In such circumstances, the group wins and the people win. Period.

It is that beautifully simple.

Like most beautifully simple things in life, however, it grows complex when humans try to actually do it. We're not even close in the West, and business has evolved into a bunch of white guys, aged between 40 and 60, who have got a nice firm grip on the *cojones* of power and see no reason to abandon their position.

More scary is the notion that they believe they're probably right to hang on.

So we're in a mess. As the legendary Dublin cab driver once said (after a fair amount of thought) when asked street directions by a tourist: "If I were you, I wouldn't start from here."

The goal of an open meritocracy is clear and attractive to all but the most lemonhead bigot, but somehow we've lost our way badly on the journey, and our "starting position" is now difficult. That in itself creates a new breed of problems:

- Cultural diversity becomes a platform for the culture that's been most offended on the journey so far, or the one that's the most vociferous. In the U.S. you don't have to choose, African-Americans win on both counts. (Although a case could be made for Native Americans having had an even worse deal. They were here first and lost everything.)

  I'd better state my position here, because the water starts getting choppy now: I'm a white male; the system threw me up as a power broker, and I've recruited or promoted a lot more white males than members of any other cultural group in my time. That does not mean I'm racist, that I accept the status quo, or that I do not want a better deal for African-Americans in all aspects of business.

  It also doesn't mean I believe that racism has disappeared; in fact, I am daft enough to believe it may be more than alive and well. It's not far beneath the thin veneer of quasi-constitutionalism and musket-nationalism that purports to be the populist movement of the moment—and remember, a lot of these Wyatt Earp/Rambo wannabes work Monday through Friday. And some of them run departments.

  Cultural diversity cannot just be about this one dimension—it must also be about the input and interest of youth and maturity, of male and female, of national and international, of Theory X and Theory Y, of able and disabled, of high-tech and low-tech, and of different experiences and religions, various languages and attitudes. If it isn't, it becomes *part of the problem, not the solution.*

- There's a second problem just as funky as that one. We've evolved into the mess we're in but, understandably, the offended parties don't want to evolve out of it; that would be way too slow.

That situation implies a program of overcorrection in the short term, involving measurable progress, forced processes, quotas, affirmative action, and protection of some "cultures" at the expense of others. What happens is that we all forget about the goal of an open meritocracy because we all become focused on getting really upset about the issues arising from managing overcorrection. Positions harden, trenches get dug, and—presto—we highlight the problems of diversity, not the benefits.

Nobody I know has a monopoly of wisdom on this subject, and I get confused and frustrated with the best of them. I do believe the following charter should *never be written down*, but that everybody in a company should memorize it:

This company will become an open meritocracy. We are not one today. (Author's note: This applies to all companies. Trust me on this one.)

We have evolved into this unhappy position, and we will evolve out of it. But we will not delay, and if we can find good shortcuts, we will use them. There is no law that says we can't evolve out of the mess a lot faster than we evolved into it.

But we will not knowingly take bad business decisions on the way.

Our open meritocracy will mean all our unrestricted mix of people contributing to their full potential for the benefit of the company and themselves.

Yes, everybody. And everybody has a job to do in this. You can be part of the problem or the solution.

And everyone will have a mentor to monitor this and nothing else.

This is part of planetary life where your God can't look back with a lot of satisfaction, or forward with much more optimism. It is a hugely complex task to get to a better state because it means we all have to discard the crap we were born without but pick up on the way: bigotry, fear, defensiveness, paranoia, and intolerance. In the political and social world there is evidence to suggest things are getting worse, not better. Maybe business can lead the way, but I would suggest you do not sit on a hot stove while you wait for it to happen.

It does sound like a songwriting challenge for Sting. (Or Pink Floyd? Hmmm . . .)

Leadership and Management

I will follow you if you'll follow me

Introduction

A while ago I found myself in a large room, crowded with a company's middle management, listening to a speech from the big cheese.

The theme was one I suspect to be common in business today. Times had been tough; sales had been soft. Profits hadn't come up to forecast levels. Managers had been through a lot together. It was going to be different from now on.

The CEO told us that the outlook was bright. He illustrated his points with large colored graphs, all of which had lines pointing upward to the right.

As a business, we were about to "turn round."

The folks in the room were all with him as his rhetoric built up to a great climax. His voice echoed around the room: "We will rise again." He paused dramatically. "We will rise again *like Spartacus from the ashes.*"

Spartacus?

I froze in disbelief. I closed my eyes and silently prayed to and for the missing Phoenix. I opened them ready to join in the furor at this silly mistake.

Forget it.

Folks were cheering. Woowoowoos of support penetrated the general enthusiastic bedlam. An attempted Mexican Wave saw warm white wine spilled on my jacket sleeve.

Something strange occurred to me. Not only did it not matter that Spartacus had been mistakenly substituted for the Phoenix, in these circumstances it was actually *better.* Images of Kirk Douglas, athletic bodies, just causes, muscles, sex, and Hollywood were much more appropriate for the task at hand.

The speaker was home dry. The audience was in his hands. I was in the presence of a *leader.*

Just what is this thing called leadership? Why is it some folks—seemingly ones without the necessary talent—prove to have it by the bucketful? Others, who seem to be so gifted, show themselves unable to lead anybody or anything out of a wet paper bag?

How does a sheepdog get the flock to where he wants it to go *without ever going in front?*

In soccer, a general belief is that you can be trained to play 10 out of the 11 positions. Given basic fitness, dedication, and technical practice, you can perform in all positions but the goalscorer. Goalscorers were born with something special, and if you haven't got it, you never will have it.

> **Management is a profession; leadership is a condition.**

Leadership and management are different, of that I've no doubt. But it is too easy to fall back on the soccer analogy; I believe leaders can be made as well as born.

I've looked at leadership for a long time, and the more I know the less I understand. I'm pretty sure of one critical distinction: Management is a *profession;* leadership is a *condition.*

These seven essays explore how this dichotomy exists. The cast is impressive, if nothing else.

On Leadership
And the possible role of Spam

Oh, my. How time flies. I cannot believe it is more than 50 years since D-day.

Watching the recent commemorations (author's factoid: It took more British and American Armed Forces staff officers to organize these events than it did for the actual invasion of Europe in 1944), my mind couldn't help but wander back to those tense, challenging times.

It seems like only yesterday that I was cooped up in a tiny, underground bunker, deep below southern England, pouring over maps of Western Europe with General Bernard Law Montgomery—"Monty" to his admirers, "Bernie" to a few very close friends.

I should say here that my close relationship with Bernie caused many eyebrows to be raised inside the Allied Military Establishment, but he invariably sought me out for his important moments and seminal decisions. I was the youngest commissioned officer in the history of any of the Allied Forces, and he saw me as the voice of what he called the new thinking and as a good foil for his feisty conservatism.

The room was lit by only a single bulb and was bitterly cold as, together, we put the final touches to the complex plan to invade Europe. "It is all in place, Bawwy. Every tiny detail," he whispered, rubbing his eyes with exhaustion. (A little author's note here: I know, 50 years later, it is politically incorrect to say so, but that tiny speech impairment that he had, and what it did to the pronunciation of my given name, pissed me off. Big-time. But I'm OK with it now. I've matured a lot.)

We looked at each other, deeply aware of the history of the moment. As we sipped our hot, sweet tea, I was able to study the man—perhaps the greatest military leader of modern times. What made him so . . . so *different*? So *capable*? He was a true leader, one of the few who commanded the respect of his troops, even when they knew his main business was to oversee programs that tragically few of them would live to talk about.

Nothing ventured, nothing gained. I took advantage of the moment and asked him what he thought made a great leader, and his response still causes me to pause and reflect to this day.

"I know I am thought of as a gwate leader of men, Bawwy, but I fear I am the last of a kind. Several thousand years ago, the Chinese army invented hierarchy and a style of leadership where one layer of hierarchy barked, just like a dog, at the next layer down. Eventually the job got done. That style hasn't changed much, at least in principle, for the armed forces of the world, or, for that matter, for the way fathers try to run families. It is also still the way most captains of industry try to run companies. As a style, it has served us well, but it has served its time."

I remember I was sort of bored by then and idly moving a model battleship up the English Channel on the table map. I was making a mental note that we must get some better scale models, because the ship was bigger than Holland,* when he suddenly raised his voice and blasted me out of my daydream.

"Do you know why you are *weally* here? Why I share all my innermost thoughts and moments with you?" I started to shape a suitably modest reply, but he just thundered on: "Because you, *you*, are tomorrow, just as I am yesterday. Armies, families, and companies will need new leaders, with new skills, as we settle into the new Golden Age after this great conflict. It may take the rest of this century, but it will come to pass."

I remember being stunned at the time. New skills? *Skills*? I didn't think leadership was about skills; I had assumed it was about a natural talent, a gift from a God. I told him so.

"Poppycock," he roared. "They all say that. My mate Charlie De Gaulle [he said this with a straight face] wrote about something he called 'instinct' that he felt all leaders must have, and Alexander called it his 'stars'—but I think Caesar was much nearer the mark when he called it 'luck.' That's a great help if you can get it, but the real skills of leadership are tangible and, in the future, will be built around processes and relationships. I have some of them, developed almost unknowingly, but I am glad my time is now.

"Leadership will become much more complex, and it may need a great guru to spread the word—probably during the last decade of this century." With that, he looked me straight in the eye.

We carried on talking well into the small hours of the morning.

---

*I have since found out that the model was right. The ship *was* bigger than Holland.

I learned from him how he thought barking skills would be superseded by influencing skills. How trust must become part of a leader's skill portfolio, manifesting itself in relationships through delegation and empowerment. How innovation and change must be enjoyed, not dreaded. And much, much more.

> **Trust must become part of a leader's skill portfolio, manifesting itself in relationships through delegation and empowerment.**

His thesis has been surely proved. But as I reflected on it, I feel he undersold himself—which was not a common fault of his (this was a man who once started a speech to his troops with the immortal words: "As God once said, *and I think quite rightly* . . ."). He was, quite possibly, the first of what *Fortune* magazine, in the 1990s, has named the "Post Heroic" leaders.

There are still too few.

My last memory of the evening was the Great Man sleeping at his table of work. Times were hard for all of us, and I quietly reached over and stole his uneaten portion of Spam, and I remember thinking then that he ate an awful lot of that fine product.

I began to wonder . . .

15

Leadership Models

Wayne, Wayne, go away

Many people believe I've passed my useful shelflife: some mentally, some physically, some both. Little do they know I still play a neat game of soccer. I am the self-confessed *libero* for Botticelli Trattoria's fine, culturally diverse, young side here in south Florida. We play Sunday mornings on any pitch we can find. Sometimes we have to finish the game on another one. A lot depends on the local police.

We play entertaining stuff, albeit we are a bit thin when it comes to crowd support. I was surprised, therefore, when Wayne Huizenga phoned up with an offer to buy the team for $165 million. We refused, naturally. The man has to be stopped somewhere. He already owns all the other quality south Florida sports teams.

But it got me thinking about leadership again, and developing some of the ideas I first shaped with Monty in 1944.

Just what will be the role model for corporate leadership in the first years of the twenty-first century? Will it be the Huizenga/Rupert Murdoch kind of model—capitalism's *arrivistes* gradually, inexorably, taking over their school playgrounds?

Or will a more sensitive model thrive, such as Bob Haas of Levi Strauss, Ben and Jerry of ice cream fame, or Anita Roddick of Body Shop? There are folks who wrestle to recognize the interests of the many stakeholders in a business, sometimes upsetting the more conventional ones by seeming to overconcern themselves with the others.

Maybe Richard Branson's "Virgin version" comes through—a style that bravely insists on trying to run a huge corporation like a mom and pop store. (That's a compliment, by the way. I was delayed once, in the U.S., on a Virgin trans-Atlantic flight. Within an hour, all of us received a fax from England, signed by him, personally apologizing and explaining what had gone wrong while telling us what Virgin was going to do to make the pain easier. I may have been delayed four hours, but I was *impressed*. Forget HFH [see essay #6]. Is that inspired leadership, or what?)

The good news—and the bad news—is that any or all of these models can and will still be around as we step nervously into the next millenium. But I believe a pattern for successful leadership is beginning to emerge, and that the true leaders in the future will have some common elements in their makeup.

- They will have exceptional *vision*. For true leaders, there is a gap at the horizon between the earth and the sky, and in that gap they alone see shapes: what their business might look like in the future, what the trading environment might be, and the possible seminal developments in their industry. They have 20–20 vision, which is not an eyesight test criterion, but a feel for what life could be in the year 2020. Seeing these shapes will be a critical element of the new leadership because they will be on their own.

Nobody else sees 'em, and to the leader will fall the task of making sure the day-to-day animated, constipated, and regulated activity in the firm supports the vision somehow.

- Leaders must have a genuine post-Copernican view of the customer (forget market, think customer). Copernicus was the guy who, in 1543, cheerfully proposed that the earth was not the center of the universe but just one of many planets circling the sun, thus blowing up the kind of thinking that still prevails with many organizations and their leaders. Many cling to the belief that they are the center of things, and the customer is within their magnetic field (until recently this was called IBM-Think), but *all* the leaders I mentioned at the start of this essay are truly post-Copernican in their understanding of where their firms fit in the customers' universe. Murdoch and Branson may have a very different approach to business, but they understand that they orbit the customer. Forever.

- Leadership will also be about *balance.* There is no option now: The firm must understand and accept that it has a whole range of stakeholders and that they all (somehow) add value and should all be rewarded (somehow) when the returns from that value adding are distributed. It is not a new idea, but it is still seen as a discretionary one, and future leaders will recognize it is no longer discretionary. As ever, the true leaders will see the problem as an opportunity, and the Body Shop's journey will not have been in vain.

- Now here's a curve ball. *Trust* will be an important ingredient in the future leadership mix. Most business leaders, when they look back over their successes and failures, can ally most of them to the people they put in charge (leaders rarely do anything).

  Putting someone in charge necessitates trust, which happens daily in business to an immensely varying degree: Some leaders find it easy, some find it the hardest thing. Some (as ever) talk a good game but then let go of little authority to go with the delegation of responsibility. Real delegation—and I'm talking about the *delegated ability to fail*—implies real trust, and if you do that the successes are resoundingly more successful. Your failures, unfortunately, are the exact opposite. But, when you add it all up, the total score is better, and there are some positive side effects.

  There have been a lot of virulent diseases on this planet, from the great plagues of history to the modern day nightmare of AIDS. Little is written, or understood, about the opposite kind of force—one that spreads health and well-being. Strange thing, trust: You trust somebody in a firm (in other words, genuinely delegate) and what happens? Maybe that person starts to do the same thing to others, and then it spreads. Before you know it, everybody's got the "disease," and you have a different kind of firm on your hands—bright, honest, open, empowered, and effective. And all that starts with leadership.

Vision. A post-Copernican view of the customer. Balance. Trust. These are the leadership "must haves" for the next century. Don't leave home without 'em, if you're serious.

> **V**ision. A post-Copernican view of the customer. Balance. Trust. These are the leadership "must haves" for the next century.

Must stop now. The guys in the team have just figured out what $165 million is divided by 11, and we've decided to sell. I mean, why should *we* be different? Must ring Wayne back and do the deal.

And start conversations about getting me under the salary cap.

Leaders: Nasty or Nice?

Smile as you downsize

I am the current darling of the cocktail set on both sides of the Atlantic. A by-product of this has seen me establish a world record 672 different alcoholic drinks that include cranberry juice.

Each party seems much the same: A hardbody (sometimes a woman) maneuvers me into a quiet corner, usually by the bulimia bucket, and asks me straight out: "Aren't you the *former* chairman and CEO of the world's second-largest hamburger chain?"

I try evasion tactics, replying: "No, no. Not me. That's the *former* Barry Gibbons you want, and he's over there." I point to some short, fat, follically impaired guy on the other side of the room, all to no avail.

Trapping me with a strategically placed knee, my interrogator carries on without pause, peering quizzically over the rim of a glass: "So. You were a captain of industry. Hmmnn. You must be a really *nasty bastard*."

Charming.

But it's an attitude that captures the view of many people today: that a real leader in modern corporate life must actually relish the ugly side of power and status— the lying, cheating, and (above all) the crushing of anything and anybody that appears as a threat. The kind of person who, if they were on a ship that ran into trouble, would gleefully drown small children, cheerfully trample pregnant women, and laughingly throw the disabled overboard to reach the lifeboat first. Real NBs (nasty bastards).

Well, I dunno. I've met a lot of these leader figures over the years and have gotten to know some of them well. Frankly, they mirror the bell curve of most human groups. There are few (if any) genuine, full-pedigree NBs, just as there are few unqualified NGs (nice guys or gals).

What makes the real leaders different is that the *circumstances* in which they operate cause them to highlight aspects of their character and/or behave in ways that can give off high NB signals, particularly to certain audiences. Perhaps the most evident of these is that all real leaders demonstrate Machiavellianism *more than most*.

Today, business needs to undergo big changes, fast just to survive—and most people don't like big, fast, change. Particularly when they talk about it together. Writing in Florence in 1513, Niccolò Machiavelli shaped theories on the craft of ruling and the exercise of power that have remained relevant for business leadership. They are also not that far off what goes on in most schools and families. Digest these words from *The Prince*, written nearly 500 years ago:

> *There is nothing more difficult to take in hand, more peril-ous to conduct, or more uncertain in its success, than to take the lead in the introduction of a new order of things. Because the innovator has for enemies all those who have done well*

under the old conditions, and lukewarm defenders who may do well under the new.

To meet and beat this problem, to get the whole business to the better place, leaders have to be forceful:

Hence it is that all armed prophets have conquered, and unarmed ones have been destroyed.

It is simply a more pointed version of a common approach to much in general life. Remember "you have to be cruel to be kind"? That wasn't Niccolò, it was usually my mom. The real leader recognizes resistance has to be beaten and tough decisions made. Both of those can get you a high NB rating.

Remember: Good leaders relate to the *whole* organization, not just a part. Modern businesses are often a complex commonwealth of vendors, producers, employees, distributors, agents, and stockholders. If you get a leader with a high NB rating and look at the organization closely, you'll often find that the reputation stems from just one interested group—often, ironically, the most vociferous but least important. I refer, of course, to the fatcat corporate staffers, who are stout defenders of the status quo because they've the most to lose and with a view that their importance is directly related to their central location.

> **Good leaders relate to the *whole* organization, not just a part.**

It is often these people who set the rumors going, the e-mail wires humming, and who leak to the press. The rest of the corporate stakeholders view the same leader as tough but fair, but to the loudmouth corporate staffer we're talking NB: an all star, Pro-Bowl, Nobel Prize–winning NB.

Good leaders don't hide, and that doesn't always help their NB rating either. People to lay off? Vendors to fire? Agencies to lose your account? Old friends who grew up with you in the company to be let go (or, worse sometimes, to be told they didn't get the big job)? Stockholders to be told bad news? There are good times and bad times to delegate, and these are bad times.

Big, nasty decisions are an everyday part of corporate life, and are usually made by the leader. Good leaders will brief big, nasty decisions personally, or make sure they're around immediately afterward. That means taking the time for one-on-one conversations or walking the floor in a troubled part of the business. It means listening to anger and sadness, and it means associating yourself with the bad news. It is easy for this stuff to associate itself with you if this aspect of leadership is important to you. And it should be.

Justified or not, do these guys actually sleep at night when they've done this stuff? I will answer only for myself, the rest you'll have to get at your own cocktail parties.

No, you do not sleep every night, but you sleep most. No, your conscience is never squeaky clean, but you know what your motives were, and you know you set out to treat people the way you would wish to be treated should the position be reversed.

And you know that the sun will come up on everything and everybody tomorrow, and you know for a fact that none of this stuff will get any easier.

I'll take a gin and cranberry juice, please. With a dash of steak sauce.

That's new drink number 673, I think.

On Handling Dissent

Jaw jaw? Or war war?

My head, of course, says it mustn't be, but my heart is fully supportive of the *fatwah* on Salman Rushdie.

I already had my suspicions, and they were more than borne out when the two of us had supper together recently, which turned out to be a complicated and clandestine affair organized jointly by the CIA and MI5. I hesitate to think of the expense to the taxpayers of both countries, but the only place we could meet was in New York City, and the only way we could make it happen was to take over Dhavat, Madhur Jaffrey's wonderful Indian restaurant.

The place itself and the road outside were obviously closed to the public for the evening.

It took but a few minutes to confirm that Rushdie is now small-minded, self-opinionated, full of his own importance and fully deserving the wrath of the whole world.

The *fatwah*, of course, is simply a rather extreme means of handling dissent, but I suppose I must bow to the Christian/democratic creed that even if I disagree with what you say, I should be prepared to die to defend your right to say it. This relegates the *fatwah* to a limited role in society, such as sorting out the tribal tensions in English soccer.

Handling dissent is a big issue today in business, with work forces probably more alienated than at any time in history. Increasingly vigilant stockholders and pressure groups of all shapes and sizes are also ready to join the attack.

Dissent can appear in groups of five or right across mighty corporations, and it can range from conversationally polite to really nasty—up to and including threats on the very lives of leaders.

Scary? Maybe. But how you respond to it and manage it represents one of the most powerful tools available to the team (corporate) leader to *improve* internal relationships and the workplace climate.

Consider the extreme, but sadly not unheard of, example in which employees are so alienated that it all boils over and personal threats—maybe even a death threat—are issued to a leader. Now a death threat in such circumstances is either a loud cry for help or . . . a death threat.

There are, broadly, two ways for the leader to respond to this unfortunate set of circumstances—apart, that is, from wondering why they don't teach *this* in business school. The first, and most popular, is to bring in expensive security consultants and have your open-plan office bombproofed, your home turned into a fortress, your workplace inundated with extensive security procedures, and your wardrobe enhanced as you wear a bulletproof vest under your coat. I figure that if it is a genuine death threat, it's unlikely that any of these tactics will stop it.

But if it is a cry for help—*as it is in approximately 100 percent of all recorded instances*—*this crap just adds gasoline to the fire.*

Leadership is about some gambles, so take one. Get everybody together. Tell 'em if they really want to harm you, you'll be easily available as you're getting rid of all security procedures immediately. Ask them to consider two things. First, if they get found out, they may pay a heavy price and, second, wouldn't it be more effective before they do the act to tell you what the deep-seated problem is and *give you a chance to fix it*?

Therein is the key to responding to, and managing, dissent: Get into conversation, be seen to get into conversation, and stay in conversation. Clearly, not everyone can get what they want, but the process itself can turn alienation into respect. As an approach it can bring dramatic results. In South Africa, Mandela and De Klerk somehow brought about democracy, in an amazingly short time span, where previously there had only been entrenched apartheid. Israel and Palestine are in conversation, incredibly, about peace and a homeland for the refugees. Few people outside the British Isles and Ireland know the real issues, emotions, and short-fuse sensitivities involved in Northern Ireland, but there is real optimism that a framework for peace is now being drawn up.

> The key to responding to, and managing, dissent: get into conversation, be seen to get into conversation, and stay in conversation.

Of course, just getting into conversation isn't enough; you'll probably find many former leaders have been there before you. To achieve a breakthrough you probably need to follow three or four laws:

- Be prepared to talk with people you do not respect, maybe even whom you despise. Possibly hate. Cut the emotion and prejudice out; your opponents have a point of view, so listen.
- Jointly understand that others, sometimes those on the sides you are representing, may wish to sabotage the outcome. Anything you achieve is likely to be too much for one side and not enough for the other. Agree to manage any sabotage together, and agree to that before it occurs.

> **Be prepared to talk to people you don't respect.**

- Calmly talk about the future; don't scream rhetoric about the past. The latter is what got you into an entrenched position, and it's unlikely to get you out. Find some new joint goals that don't seek total victory but give shape to a better state of peace.
- Think carefully about facilitators and arbitration. Then don't use either.

Getting negotiations right can be such a powerful weapon that many organizations now institutionalize dissent by constantly seeking counterpoints of view and managing the process that comes out of it. The name for that is *challenge culture*, and for once I'm not cynical about a fancy new name. It's probably the healthiest corporate culture there is.

There is another way, of course. The mid-nineties witnessed a U.S. major league baseball strike, giving us the new Beavis and Butthead process for managing dissent. When it's finally over, you'll probably see some nice, brightly colored, bulletproof vests worn over some players' uniforms.

Particularly by Salman Rushdie, who is currently a relief pitcher for the Yankees. Oops! I don't think I should have said that.

Leaders' Pay

Did he *really* say Meg Ryan?

My compensation package, in my last year as a Captain of Industry, is a matter of certified public record, and I summarize it here without any reticence. I have rounded all figures to the nearest $100,000:

- My basic salary was $823.7 million (with a 12-year Notice of Termination clause).
- Stock option gains during the year totaled $2.659 billion.
- Appropriate housing was provided by the company in Florida, Munich, Sydney, and Osaka, with a quaint "strategic retreat" just next to the king's private train station and golf course in Hua Hin, on the coast south of Bangkok.
- Three Gulf Stream jets were at my disposal, 24 hours a day, with a smaller jet on call for my two golden retrievers (fitted with a golden fire hydrant).
- I also had a 60-foot-long limo, driven by a recent Miss Universe, together with matching platinum Range Rovers for all members of my family.

- Fifteen new Armani suits a month were made available, together with unlimited Ralph Lauren spectacles. I liked the ones that make you look like a Japanese prisoner of war camp commandant. They make me look suitably serious when I appear on "Larry King Live."
- A weekly pedicure, often given by Meg Ryan.

Looking back, two thoughts cross my mind: *Where did it all go* and, I can understand the less privileged classes in business (or "pond scum" as we joyfully called them during our Executive Committee strategic retreats in Rio) wondering if any one person could be worth all that.

It is a debate that rages in business today all over the Western world.

During a recent visit to England I witnessed the AGM of one of the top 10 public companies being disrupted by stockholders (representing 50 million shares) angry at the salary package of the Fatcat (their words) running the company. The proposal that he resign, however, was outvoted by the *two billion shares* held by the institutions that didn't turn up but voted by proxy. Their view was simple: Ol' Fatcat added value.

A soccer team in the UK was stranded at the bottom of the league midway through this last season, and the board of directors did what boards have done in all walks of sport, business, and life in general: They fired the head guy. Under a new boss, the team (with no new players) suddenly started to win, avoided relegation, and won one of the two English trophies at the end of the season. To my sure knowledge nobody complained about the new guy's top-end compensation; in fact, the common view was that it was a bargain. Whatever it was.

This phenomenon is the core of the debate. Whether it is true or not (and there is enough evidence to suggest *it just could be true*), we believe in miracle workers—people who will succeed with a given set of resources, and in a given set of circumstances, where virtually nobody else can.

If things are going wrong, the pressure and the temptation to fire the guy in place and seek a miracle worker is almost irresistible. You are seen to be doing something dramatic and, hey, it might just work. The question of what you can afford to pay is irrelevant; you can't afford not to appoint one of these guys. And if you've got one already, you can't afford to lose him or her.

The reality is that these people are unique, but this is not just about their inherent skills or talents. They come in all shapes, sizes, and decibel levels, but they have that indeterminable common *something* that seems to give the organization, and its people, its necessary vitamins and nutrients.

Take time and study the story of a boyhood hero of mine: Tony O'Reilly, onetime Irish rugby star, then meteoric business success, now head of the mighty Heinz empire and a handful of worldwide businesses in communications, finance, and manufacturing. He's one of the megaearners and I have no idea whether he's worth it in a world where we pay teachers with loose change yet offer a $100 million basketball contract to a kid just coming out of college (albeit a kid who happens to have eaten his spinach and grown to seven feet tall).

What I do know is that business is risky, frustrating, and complex, like climbing a steep hill covered in loose stones and rocks. Something weird happens if you get the right person in charge (whether it is a team or a company). Suddenly everybody feels surefooted and begins to climb with confidence. Those same guys in that soccer team felt that new presence and suddenly passed more accurately, shot straighter, and found faith in themselves.

That's what you pay for.

When it works, no price is too expensive—and don't spend too long on the debate because while it works it's here to stay, however amoral it may appear. We pay some weird prices for freedom, like biting our tongues when people burn our national flags or doing nothing when others march in Ku Klux Klan or Nazi uniforms. Not to mention Howard Stern.

> **The price of anything must be set where the demand line crosses the supply line.**

The price of anything must be set where the demand line crosses the supply line on the graph. Imperfect, maybe, but history has proved it better than any other system. Long may it reign.

Oh. I forgot. I also had a clause in my contract that provided for free Whoppers for my two teenage sons. For IRS purposes, that was valued at $17.6 million for my last full year.

19

Leading Simply and Leading Right

And Alexander the Great's great thirst

James Taylor's "Sweet Baby James" was the surreal lullaby for a generation, but not many realize that he wrote it to celebrate the birth of my first son.

It was mildly unfortunate that his name was Jon, but those were heady days. James wasn't much into details at the time. It was, nevertheless, a neat gesture and does nothing to explain why our friendship drifted over the years. I managed, however, to catch him at a concert recently, and he was still impressive on stage—languid and sinewy, fronting a nice tight band, serving up all the required anthems but peppering the steak nicely with some relevant new stuff. The guy still writes a curve ball into a lyric as well as anyone.

Even more impressive was the content of a recent speech of his. Invited to address an audience full of music students while he accepted an honorary degree, James faced them from the podium and solemnly pronounced: "Keep your overhead low, stay off drugs, play every day." Then he made his exit.

Exactly 10 words serve as a lesson for everyone operating in business today; they are short, clear, and relevant. They also provide a magnificent combination of *a charter of values, a mission statement, an ethics code, and an operating manual.*

The virulent disease symptomized by the spread of these documents is now of near epidemic proportions. Millions of dollars and hours, and thousands of "specialists" and agencies are now employed in getting these wordy statements just right.

Boardrooms all over the Western world echo with self-serving drivel such as, "Everybody in our organization must know what our values are, what we stand for, where we are going, and why we are whithering." No! Stop! I apologize—that last bit was mine. I couldn't resist!

As a process of thought, of course, all this is fine; the problems come with the inability to resist the temptation to write it down, frame it, and put it on the wall in the cafeteria.

The morning I first arrived at Burger King was tense. That scion of Americana had just been bought by the British company I worked for via a vigorously contested acquisition, and as I walked into the rather palatial corporate headquarters a lot of cold, vanquished eyes were looking at me as though I represented some remote conquering planet.

I found my office, went inside, and began the long walk to my desk (which, I think, doubled as a heliport, judging from its size). Pretty much all documentation had been removed except for one framed jewel on the wall: the previous company's mission and values statement.

What a crock it was—a rambling, shambling mumbo-jumbo of unnecessary adverbs, self-deluding rhetoric, and split infinitives, and the irony of it gave me my first grin of the day. *If they'd have lived by half of what was in that frame, I wouldn't have been there.*

It was then and there that I figured out that you can write and publish what you want, but the only missions, values, and ethics that count in your company are those that manifest themselves in the behavior of all the people, all the time. And when I say all the people, I mean all the people, but particularly those with leadership responsibilities at any levels.

> The only missions, values, and ethics that count in your company are those that manifest themselves in the behavior of all the people, all of the time.

Alexander the Great had much in common with Margaret Thatcher; they were both being fine examples of the need for limited terms of office for the highest leaders.

Like Thatcher, Alexander was a magnificent leader in his first years of power, but he lost it as he drifted away from reality, began to believe his spin-doctors, and gradually convinced himself he was a god. But the prime years were something special and contain any number of examples of the point I'm making, the best being an incident during a forced desert march with his army, with water running desperately short.

A foot soldier approached the Great One with some of the precious liquid he'd saved from his own ration and offered it to him (thus proving that attempting to crawl your way to promotion is *not* a new idea). Alexander paused and asked the man whether he had enough water for 10,000 men. On being told no, Alexander slowly poured it into the sand.

I wasn't there (that would be stretching it, even for me), but I can tell you exactly what happened next. There were no electronic communications, but within two hours every soldier would have known about that incident. Huddled around their fires in the cold desert night, there would have been but one topic of conversation: It was a pig of a mission they were on, lives would be lost, but they were all in it together and they had the right guy leading them.

Not a guy who is clever and nice with words in the annual report but who runs an organization that has nasty people doing nasty things all over the place. And not a guy who preaches about the difficulties of job losses and cost cutting but who travels in a stretch limo to the bathroom and dines most days on pan-fried pigeon breasts nestling in a lightly dressed green salad washed down with Dom Perignon.

Remember James Taylor; keep it simple. Then make sure you act, and everybody else acts, off the same script. If you have to articulate this stuff, get it into fewer than 10 words like the Allies did in 1944, with their collective mission being simply agreed as, "We will take Berlin." That was all that was needed for the purpose. The timing, place, cast, and tactics can all follow later, at a different level.

> A good starting point is the courtesy, common sense, and sensitivity to others you are born with, and which the world slowly beats out of most people.

If you then feel the need to get there with a cool set of values and ethics, you would do well to remember that a good starting point for both is the courtesy, common sense, and sensitivity to others you are born with, and which the world slowly beats out of most people.

You don't need to write anything down because it is still there inside the majority and is keen to get out. It actually makes for a nicer day. So lead by example and make it a way of life for everybody in your company, and, yes, openly celebrate good examples and quietly come down heavily on the opposite.

And all this from a few words of James Taylor.

Fairly shortly, I will attempt a treatise inspired by the lyrics of Snoop Doggy Dog. I, for one, simply cannot wait.

Managing Disaster

Oh, about your cherry tree—
he chopped it down

As I tenderly approach my fiftieth birthday, I have this calling to confess past crimes.

I was personally responsible for one of the great marketplace disasters of the century. As the sixties were ending their roller coaster ride, Bobby (to his friends) Dylan and I were at the height of our creative relationship, partying, singing, and writing together almost as one.

One time, in the wee small hours of the morning, in a scruffy dressing room backstage in some club in Madrid, we were really flowing. We'd spent the evening smoking something antisocial (although we didn't inhale) and were attempting a nightcap cocktail based on sherry and the oil used on English cricket bats, when it suddenly came to me.

I looked him straight in the eye he had open, and told him: "I think you should go *electric.*"

He agreed, and fell off the couch. The resulting disaster is now part of history. His switch from acoustic ranked, in catastrophe terms, slightly above the forced Perrier market withdrawal of a few years later and right alongside Hugh Grant's unfortunate incident. Bobby's fans deserted him, and he never wrote a song of substance again. He lost all articulation and began squeaking strangely through his nose. TwoWestern governments fell, and the peso collapsed. There is, however, some evidence to suggest that Dylan was not entirely responsible for the latter.

The management of such fun happenings in business as the genuine market catastrophe is a strangely neglected science.

It is a living evocation of the maxim that "It surely couldn't happen here." It is as though even talking about it or planning for it on a contingency basis is tempting fate just that teeny bit too much.

Which brings me to Mercedes. With a couple of notable exceptions, I admit upfront that I do not have a deep love affair with people and things of German origin.

But I have respect for German business and know Mercedes to be a fine brand by any definition, which makes the next bit ever so strange.

At the start of the 90s Mercedes launched its "S" class car, a heavyweight both literally (at more than 4,500 lbs) and financially (costing up to $100,000). Complaints about the cars—specifically, about them vibrating badly—grew and grew until eventually a class action suit appeared on behalf of some 2,000 shaking customers.

Mercedes's response to all this? Apparently the firm handed it to a corporate ostrich who put his head in the sand and addressed these people through his butt, telling them *they were all wrong!* The implication was that they were imagining it or making it up.

What brilliance! Now, I don't know about you, but if I've spent $100,000 on a car and it is shaking the glass out of my wristwatch, I do not want my integrity challenged when I mention it to the manufacturer.

But let's forget about the merits of luxury cars for a moment because they are not actually important here; let's talk instead about *effects.* Do you know what I think happened next? I think 2,000 existing Mercedes customers pencilled in Lexus as their next buy, and maybe 5,000 (10,000? 100,000?) potential customers started thinking Jaguar or Cadillac. This story was published on the front page of *The Wall Street Journal.*

The real problem wasn't the problem; the problem was the *response* to the problem.

Now consider Carnival Cruise lines and its nightmare with the liner *Ecstasy* losing all power at sea. A grim time ensued until Carnival could transfer the passengers to another vessel, but then the company responded so positively (granting travelers an extra free day, money back, future goodies, and—brilliant thinking—a free bar) that by the time the ship docked, the company scored an 84 percent approval rating from the people on board.

There are two basic rules here:

- When you get that sickening call that informs you that disaster has struck your company or brand, you must have somebody—or a process—in place that can *accept* the fact.

  This is the hardest part: The great temptation is to somehow get into a holding pattern, to keep talking but do nothing. You desperately hope the disaster won't be so bad, will go away, or will turn out to be somebody else's fault. It's tough to ask anyone to respond with the speed that is needed when the implications can be so frightening, and all companies should have a preagreed process in which one or more decision makers *of the right stature* are accessible 24 hours every day.

You should also rapidly get your top corporate lawyers together, listen to them intently, and then *ignore* everything they say. This issue is about leadership. If you can accept it fast (a basic oxymoron to the legal profession), however horrible it is, you've a chance of coming out with an 84 percent approval rating.

- The second rule can only come into play when the first one is behind you. It is to treat the next process as though it was being paid for out of your *advertising* budget. When companies advertise, they are paying to reach an audience with a message about their products and, indirectly, about themselves. You can be sure a disaster will get an audience without your spending a single dollar for media—and that audience will include existing and potential customers, employees, suppliers, and stockholders.

  Your product has taken a hit, but it has presumably been caused by a freak set of circumstances. People do understand that. How you respond will say more about what kind of company is behind your products than any advertising money you could spend, so don't whine, don't hide, and don't dodge responsibility.

- If necessary take *more* than your share of responsibility and *overfix* the problem. Save the arguments for your insurance claim later.
- Don't bluff; in this kind of spotlight, bluffing can come back and bite you high on the inside leg.

Hey. I feel another confession coming on. I'm not sure I can come out into the open fully with this one. Here's a hint: It involves me making a daft bet with Marilyn Monroe and President Kennedy. Looking back, I'm really not proud of myself.

4

Organizations— and Organizing

To be or not to be?

Introduction

Some 450 years before the birth of Christ, a Greek philosopher called Empedocles defined his preferred deity as follows: "God is a circle whose center is everywhere and whose circumference is nowhere."

I have thought about this deeply and here give you my considered view. The man was a fruitcake.

That nebulous fortune cookie stuff is a solid reason why this planet is a mess. It means nothing, it means everything. It bores some, excites others.

It has been an ever-present symptom of religious writing, from way before the time of Empedocles and ever since. Philosophers and economists took up the style enthusiastically. In the last century, writers on business have really refined the art. And when these guys write about organizations, all bets are off. Substitute the words *an organization* for *God* in the previous quotation, then ask yourself how many times you've heard or read something like that recently. How about the *virtual organization*? Yeah, right. In this project, an organization is defined as a bunch of folks pursuing common interests as well as their own.

Apart from the family, the most widespread organizational model on earth is the business unit. There are millions of them, from mighty corporations spanning the globe to the tiny plumbing business you call out to fix your blocked drain. Many of them are so big, that they have many suborganizations: regions, divisions, subsidiaries, staff functions, and so on.

In a regulated political and economic system such as communism, the business organization has a social role. It is usually built around the provision of employment and the distribution of wealth. When communism failed, it was not because the organizations failed in that role, it was because the role has a San Andreas fault line built into it. It was self-destructive.

In the world of free enterprise and capitalism, the organization has a social as well as economic role. Sometimes it is accepted, albeit reluctantly. Sometimes it is rejected.

The gap between what governments are willing to provide and what the individual can provide is wide, and widening. There are a lot of growth trends at work in this gap, such as the provision of healthcare for an aging population, the incidence of drugs and violent crime, and the growing need for training and education in a high-tech world. These don't begin to mention the need to protect the planet and the consumer from commercial exploitation.

The business organization is the prime enabler for wealth creation. As such, it already plays an important social role in our system. It is under pressure, however, to step into these other resource gaps because there is no other mechanism that begins to have the capability.

Some organizations welcome this specter. They are defined as *enlightened*. That's fine by me as long as the corporations themselves aren't doing the defining.

Some hate the idea.

It is, and will remain, an uncomfortable concept for free enterprise business. In the same way as the church and the state have wrestled with their differing (but frequently overlapping and confronting) roles within our system, so will these economic and social forces have to battle it out. Governance and profit optimization are not the same thing. There are other stakeholders than just stockholders.

The model itself is changing. Big is still beautiful particularly in industries where product development costs are humongous, such as pharmaceuticals. It is also a trend where distribution economies exist and there are few geographic boundaries, such as in banking and communications.

A trend within that trend, however, is seeing companies focus on their core competencies. They are restructuring around their seminal processes and outsourcing a lot of the services they previously did inhouse. This stuff is being picked up by new, small, startup businesses.

So, as I said: An organization is a circle whose center is everywhere and whose circumference is nowhere.

OK! OK! I cheated! But I bet some of you bought it!

The next six essays explore the issues in plain English. The word *virtual* has been banned.

As for Empedocles, he eventually declared himself divine and jumped into the crater of Mount Etna in an attempt to prove it. I *told* you he was a fruitcake.

21

I Organize, Therefore I Am

Tammy Faye who?

There is never a bad time to pause for a philosophy check.

I got a wonderful chance to do that recently. I picked up the Concorde, out of London, on my way back from Japan after setting up the Pacific Rim Division of the research team for this collection of essays. They were nicely housed in premises kindly donated to us by the Osaka Institute for the Minimization of Rice Imports.

On the short, exciting flight, I was delighted to find that I sat next to my old, old friend the Dalai Lama, the exiled spiritual leader of Tibet. He had been advised by his PR team to undertake a continuous world tour to repair the damage done to his cause by Richard Gere's enthusiasm and support for it.

We settled into the journey together, and our conversation meandered over the philosophy of capitalism, wealth creation, and the organization.

He spoke in the measured, hushed style that is all his own: "Listen, Glasshopper [an old joke between us], it is written that capitalism and the organization must reinvent themselves by the turn of the millenium or die. I must now meditate, but, before I do, I will ask some questions. These questions *must* find answers, but they cannot be resolved within the status quo."

I said nothing. I had little idea of what he was talking about.

He went on: "First question. It is the perceived wisdom that capitalism has 'won,' but when you look at central and eastern Europe, capitalism has brought nothing but disaster, by any measure. *Why?*

"Next. Capitalism operates differently in Japan than in mainland Western Europe, which, in turn, operates differently from the American and British model. Yet it is all treated as the same science. *Why?*

"Third question. The idea of limited liability was the great facilitator for capitalism and the company. It is accepted today that a company has many stakeholders: producer/suppliers, distributors, retailers/franchisees/agents, employees, stockholders, neighbors, communities, fellow earthlings, and customers. Above all, customers. If the firm fails, many of these stakeholders can be devastated. Employees can lose livelihoods, Exxon caused Alaska to lose its beauty, and there is a healthy debate ranging today as to whether the tobacco giants have *knowingly* caused more deaths in their customer base than did Hitler. But only one stakeholder has limited liability. *Why?*"

The cabin seemed very quiet as he posed his final question:

"The organization has been built around something called a *job,* a one-dimensional relationship between employer and employee. Time has passed. Things are different now. Yet we have steadfastly refused to recognize that the needs of the employer are multidimensional, as are the needs of the employee. *Why?"*

He smiled; ate some rough, brown rice with three fingers; sipped his Dr Pepper; rolled his eyes round the back of his head somewhere; and was gone into a trance.

I was suddenly overcome with a feeling that I could make a major breakthrough, and I looked around the cabin for support.

Nothing.

From two seats back, Tammy Faye Bakker smiled at me warmly while scratching the side of her nose with a combat-length finger nail, but I didn't count that.

I was on my own, but almost of its own accord, my pen leapt into my hand and I began to write on my napkin. For the sake of history, I reproduce, here *exactly* what I wrote:

A catechism for an organization (check spelling when you get back).

- *A company must still work within a model of capitalism and create wealth. Enterprise and the Invisible Hand still rule, OK?*

- *An organization must no longer be just the corporation. It is a commonwealth of interests of all its stakeholders. It cannot succeed by rolling a six on the dice for one group, whereas others score a one. The chief executive's job is one of balance, striving for a four or five on all dice.*

- *In the future, the organization will report back to all stakeholders on how each has added value to the commonwealth and how each has been rewarded.*

- *There will cease to be anything called a job. The business needs within the commonwealth will be defined as a circle. The individual's needs within the commonwealth will be defined as a circle. Where the circles overlap, there will be multidimensional relationships.*

> **There will cease to be anything called a *job.***

There was a fifth point in the catechism, but I spilled Ketchup over it (I am getting very American in my habits) and couldn't remember it afterward.

When the flight ended, I couldn't wait to show the Dalai Lama my breakthrough, but there was no need. "I know *every word you have written*, Glasshopper," he smiled, "and it has wisdom beyond your years. May your God go with you."

With that, he was gone, lost in the crowd at JFK, clutching his duty-free bag.

22

The Role
of the
Organization

And a possible new flavor
for Ben and Jerry

If I'm feeling mischievous, I ask a group of MBA students who, or what, was a Nostradamus. Sometimes I ask a bunch of CEOs.

The nearest I have to a correct answer (the *nearest*, mind you) is a Ben and Jerry flavor. No matter. The truth is much less exciting, because Nostradamus was a Frenchman who wrote in the early sixteenth century. This was no ordinary writer, mind you; he devoted a big part of his life to penning about a thousand quatrains—four-line unstructured verses—that forecast the future of the world from his time until nearly the year 4000 AD. I know every one by heart, of course, and frequently entertain the crowds in John Martin's Irish bar here in Miami with impromptu renditions translated into Gaelic.

Many students, however, think that he wrote absolute drivel; others point out he has already forecast every key event that has happened in the last 500 years—the great conflicts, the natural disasters, and the rise and fall of the most famous (and infamous) characters. Not to mention Prince Charles's affair.

And that's the whole point of the stuff: reading it doesn't actually tell you what he forecast, you have to interpret it, and students have been happily kept in support grants for centuries in this exciting pursuit.

Can Nostradamus help us with figuring out what the hell to do with capitalism?

Well, while browsing through the verses the other night trying to find a reference to O. J. Simpson, I came across the following:

The feigned union will be of short duration,
Some changed, most reformed.
A new organization rises as a true flame,
Now a Ringmaster, less talk of Subjects.

Now, please bear in mind that I had to translate this from the original medieval French regional dialect (not one of my strengths), but assuming I'm there or thereabouts, this is fascinating. Trust me on this one and stop yawning.

The way you go about interpreting this stuff is to drift along a bit (da da dee dum, etc.), then pounce and concentrate on a couple of words.

The first couple of lines certainly line up with my general thesis—that capitalism worked OK for a short while. Indeed, it's seen some changes and some reforms, but now a new idea must rise. The organization must be more of a *Ringmaster*, with less talk of *Subjects*.

Let's take the last one first, and here I can only give you my scholastic view that this represents Old Nossy's assertion that organizations have largely been about employment (for *employee* read *subject*).

For sure, the company is a limited-liability vehicle for stockholders, but it's really about employment: When it grows it takes more on, when it downsizes it cuts some subjects. If the company has a mission, it has usually employed people to deliver it. CEOs are frequently seen pounding podiums yelling: "Our people are our firm's greatest asset." (Author's note: Yeah, right.)

So what's the change here? What's with the Ringmaster bit? I confess it took me a while, but I think I've got it. What Nostradamus means is that the primary role of the organization, its *raison d'etre,* is not to employ subjects but to stand in the middle of some kind of ring and conduct—or organize—a circling cavalcade of activity of vendors, distributors, agents, employees, stockholders, contractors, franchisees, licensees, and partners. And customers. And communities.

Sorry about the bit of French in the middle of the last para. Must be this red wine.

Anyway, there's a bizarre thought: An organization's role is to organize, not employ. A new generation of companies is already there. Virgin is a fine example.

> **An organization's role is to organize, not employ.**

They think it's cool to employ only a few people. They think when any part of the organization reaches about 50 (at the absolute maximum 100) subjects, it stops adding value and should self-destruct.

The point isn't about numbers employed in the organization, it's about numbers directly employed. It advocates that the vast majority of jobs are so varied that they are better contracted, or licensed, out to a work force that both needs and can provide that variety. And specialized expertise.

And it's not about profitability or earnings per share declining. In fact, quite the opposite.

Hey! I can hear a chorus from the CW3 Choir ("It can't work, won't work.")

But just ask the guys at Nintendo, who net *about $1.5 million profit per employee.* Nike doesn't even own its own production facilities. If it ain't design or marketing, it is farmed out to contractors, licensees, or partners. And more and more organizations are beginning to look like this.

The organization as a ringmaster has *big* implications for what we used to call a job (see also *career*) and for the science of workplace location and design. But right now I'm fascinated by this quatrain I've just found in the Prophesies:

Treat me right, treat me good,
Treat me like you know you should.
'Cause I'm not made of wood,
And I don't have a wooden heart.

Er, this one seems to have lost something in translation, *N'est-ce pas?*

On Social Responsibility

A United Nations charter charter

Boutros Boutros Ghali and I go way, way back. It seems like only yesterday that we were kids chasing cobras together in the foothills south of Cairo.

He was recently in South America on a UN mission to trace the correct pronounciation of *Pele* and telephoned to see whether he could drop in and have a chat as he swung through Miami on his way to New York.

Obviously, I was only too pleased and went to meet him personally at our famous international airport. It had been a few years since we last met, but I recognized him immediately as he picked his way gingerly through some chickens and goats in the main concourse.

"Hey! Boutros Boutros!" I yelled, waving frantically. "Welcome to Miami Miami!"

That was, of course, my little joke and one that he used to enjoy. But the affairs of state weigh so heavily on him these days that he barely smiled. He went straight into business, telling me that the UN World Strategy Committee had been tracking my collection of essays. Because of our special relationship, he had been sent to see whether we could work together on a draft of a particular policy paper as a matter of great urgency.

"You see, Barry Barry," he said, this time with the ghost of his old smile back, "there is a growing gap between the ability of the governments and the individuals of the world to adequately resource the social, environmental, and developmental needs of the planet and its people."

He went on, gathering pace, "Some of the needs are truly infinite. So we must look to companies, which are becoming increasingly influential and more often than not international, to play a part in bridging that gap without jeopardizing the principles of free market competition and wealth creation.

"It's a toughie, but the guys back at the UN ranch asked if you and I could knock together some sort of world charter over a working lunch."

He was limited for time, so I took him straight from the airport to one of Miami's fine gourmet Italian restaurants in Coral Gables. Luckily we were able to rent a couple of cellular phones for an hour or two so we could put them on the table. (We didn't want to draw attention to ourselves by not having any.)

I thought the challenge was exciting, and as soon as we had settled in I opened the conversation with not a little confidence: "Look, BB, I know about these things. I've been studying how big companies go about such challenges, and what we need here, to start, is a mission statement."

The effect of those words on my guest was startling. "Mission statement?" he snorted, way too loudly for some of the other diners, "mission statement? I cannot think of two words that say more about why firms have lost their way. Hey, I'll give you a mission statement for this: Just get on with it, you've absolutely no bloody choice."

I was stunned. What would my old business school say?

But BB just carried on without missing a beat. "I'm not talking about companies aggressively marketing themselves as socially responsible, although I expect that will grow as a science, and it has proved very effective for those such as Body Shop and Ben and Jerry's. I'm not talking about those firms behaving in a socially responsible way in all their spheres of influence. That's a 'must' just to defend your market position today and will probably be a must to survive in future. I'm talking about discretionary programs a company can involve itself in. For that we need a simple world charter. That is our task today."

Right there and then, amidst the cellular phones and risotto in squid's ink, we wrote it. Again, purely in the interests of history, I reproduce it here:

United Nation's Charter for the Firm's Social Responsibility Programs. We don't have what you might call an actual mission statement here, but if we did, it would be something like: Just get on with it. There is NO CHOICE.

- Don't try and do lots of things. Choose one area and focus your efforts and resources. That way you can make a difference.

- Choose an area of synergy for your firm. If you have particular skills or resources that can benefit a program, use 'em. For example, if you run a fast-food chain used to dealing with

> **Do NOT let the CEO near the decision making. Even more so, do not let the CEO's spouse near it.**

thousands of teenagers, lean toward training and education programs. If you are a food producer, help feed the hungry. There is a way in which every company can help—with the singular exception of the tobacco giants. There is nothing they can do now.

- This is not about boosting next week's sales, but it is common sense to work in areas where you can be exposed to your product's target market.

- Do *not* let the CEO near the decision making. This is not an area for hobby farming. Even more so, do not let the CEO's spouse near it. You should rather empower a small team representing all the company's stakeholders. And tell them to get on with it.

- Don't just build your program around giving money. Time (volunteerism), materials (prod-

> **When you give money, insist that it be spent professionally.**

ucts), systems (computer time, electonic mail, etc.), facilities (office space), and services (mailing, trucking, etc.) can all be invaluable to not-for-profit programs.

- When you give money, insist that it be spent professionally, that the appropriate options be analyzed and the most effective one chosen, that basic controls be in place, and that there be some review mechanism.

We finished in good time for him to get his plane, but just as we were leaving, my cellular phone rang.

Can you believe it? I'd only rented it an hour ago, and it was for me, personally.

It was, of course, CitiBank Visa, telling me that I was such a good guy that they wanted me to take advantage of its insurance and travel service programs.

Yeah, right. Or as BB said, as he got in the car laughing heartily (just like the old days): "Tell 'em to go pound sand sand."

Balancing Your Act

And other disappearing species

A number of things are disappearing from the planet earth. We are, for example, losing species at a rate that will see one-fifth of the total gone from earth within 10 years. If that includes the four-foot-long black snake that occasionally occupies my yard, that's fine by me.

The rain forests are going fast. Guns 'n Roses has split up.

The soda fountain in South Miami has closed its doors forever. (Author's note to Bill Clinton: Should Saddam Hussein ever threaten Kuwait again, just lay your hands on the counter staff from that soda fountain and send them, unarmed, to the Gulf. It will be all over in minutes.)

Another thing that is leaving us, irrevocably, is something called *balance*. It is not cool to have a balanced view on anything anymore. If it were, why would Rupert

Murdoch and a handful of other guys be gradually taking over the planet's media?

My close friend John Who?, the prime minister of Great Britain, was bemoaning his luck in our weekly Sunday afternoon telephone call. He's standing way back behind the Labour Party in the opinion polls, and he puts it down to the fact that his administration is probably too balanced for modern public tastes. By this I presume he means that for every cross dresser he has in his team, there is an equal and opposite insider dealer.

Balance has long gone from most companies, which is one reason why we are getting humongous restructuring and reengineering charges that are largely corporate attempts to rebalance.

There are two ways that a company can get out of balance. First, management can make a good, open, honest balls-up when running the business, and IBM, General Motors, Sears, Wang, Perrier, (new) Coca Cola, and a good many other examples spring to mind from the last couple of decades. The results can be hugely amusing if you're not directly involved.

The other way a company grows unbalanced is less dramatic but a bit more sinister. It can have equally spectacular results measured in lost balance.

I've worked for three major corporations and remember vividly in one of them being cheerfully directed by my boss to do what I had to do to make the actual year-end figures mirror the projected ones. It was expected that you had a tough arm wrestle with the auditors, and you must stay within generally accepted accounting principles (Whee! Such fun!), but the exact quote was: "Just look after the short-term profits. Keep doing that, and the long-term results look after themselves."

Hey. Presto. Magic.

So what happens? When a tough year comes along, you engage in a series of dumb activities, designed to flatter the Polaroid picture of the period end accounts at the expense of the entire feature-length-movie, that is, the continuing health of the company.

You all know the tricks: Cut training, marketing, and maintenance expenses; factor receivables; sell assets and book the profits (known in England as selling the family silver to pay the butler). Hold checks at the year end. Flood your customers' shelves and warehouses with your product and book the sale (usually at extreme discounts; your customers are not daft).

And there are many, many more devices. You've probably got your own special favorites.

What happens, of course, is that all these fudges come back to bite you in the leg in the next accounting period. So you find you have a bigger gap to bridge next period end, *so you do the same thing again only more so.*

And so on, and so on. Till you're really out of balance—see IBM and its cohorts mentioned earlier.

In my view, about half of most restructuring charges are simply about taking a deep breath and getting back in balance again.

> **About half of most restructuring charges are simply about taking a deep breath and getting back in balance again.**

Among the accounting and behavioral shambles that we call Western business, however, there are some clear voices of sanity. Some organizations seek better balance in returns to the many stakeholders in a firm. These firms seek to stay balanced as they address both long- and short-term goals. I recently came across this quote:

We don't define our goals in terms of annual growth rates. That is one of the great diseases of American business. We used to have a growth-oriented culture. However, the trouble

*is, if you pursue growth, you'll get it. But you'll also get . . .
badly considered investments, profitless products, and shabby
business practices.*

*We believe that if you provide a good product, provide
preeminent customer service, and create an environment in
which your people feel rewarded and fulfilled and are ener-
gized by the work, the growth and profitability will auto-
matically come.*

This was from the CEO of one of America's leading
branded companies, who will remain anonymous because
the buttheads who govern Western capitalism would
probably mark the stock price down if they knew who it was.

> **The trouble is, if you pursue growth, you'll get it. But you'll also get badly considered investments, profitless products, and shabby business practices.**

But I implore you to read it and reread it. And celebrate every word because with beacons like this, we
can reestablish balance on corporate earth at least.

To be balanced is not about losing your competitive edge. Gillette is argu-ably the best branded
business in the world, and each year the company invests
the equivalent of its operating profit in R&D. And each
year it invested the equivalent of its capital spend in marketing. You won't catch Gillette off balance.

Balance. There's a chance it is still alive and might
come back, which is fine by me.

I must go now; Oliver North is about to appear on TV.

25

Organizational Development

And the part played by aroma therapy

Let me report on my exciting recent visit to Cairo to the UN International Conference on Population and Development. Despite the opposition from the Vatican (currently exhausted from just having ratified Copernicus), candidates from 150 countries endorsed a landmark plan to curb population growth.

I like to feel I played my part, cochairing with Jane Fonda the important Subcommittee on Aroma Therapy.

A hot topic of conversation in the breakout rooms in the Cairo Holiday Inn was the modern day relevance of Thomas Malthus. You will remember that, in 1798, he wrote that the world's ability to increase food supplies was arithmetic, whereas its ability to grow its people was geometric (which means faster; trust me on this one). The resultant population surplus, Malthus proposed, would be handled by a mixture of such factors as war, famine, disease, natural disasters, and the Menendez brothers.

Two hundred years later, it's hard to argue against the guy.

Ever vigilant in my research, I began to play with the idea that similar forces might be at work in organizations.

Stop and think about companies you've known—either directly or through the media—for a long period. Management has the ability to grow revenues at an arithmetic rate of increase but also has the ability to shoot itself in the foot at something much higher than a geometric rate.

There are a whole range of creative ways of mishandling this gun, such as letting costs get bloated, losing touch with the customer, developing marketing myopia, misjudging the competition, and backing the wrong product lines. In some spectacular cases (for example, IBM motto: We built the world's heaviest airplane) all of these apply.

The results can be amazing. IBM wiped more than *$70 billion* from its market value between 1987 and 1993.

In these cases, the organizational equivalent of the Malthusian "correcting forces" is needed.

Some use the equivalents of "war," such as McDonald's, which wages war on the basis of price (oops, sorry! Value Menu!). I guess the business equivalent of "plagues" is cyclical recessions, which, although they hurt, neatly wipe out a few competitors if you're lucky.

Which leaves us to consider the organizational equivalent of the "natural disaster"—the big, one-off, overnight, traumatic readjustment, wiping out thousands of unnecessary staff. This, of course, is now known as downsizing (or reengineering, which sounds much more positive).

Is there a way of running a business, over the long haul, which avoids the need for these dramatic Malthusian elements to get you back on track? Impacting the marketplace is one way, which I talked about in section one. Here, though, I want to concentrate on keeping costs, focus, and productivity continually in shape to avoid the natural disaster of downsizing every few years.

Make no mistake: The disaster analogy is a fair one. The fact that the stock market often marks the stock up on such an occasion usually reflects that investors see it simply as a lesser disaster than the status quo.

Why disaster? In my eyes anything that signals a dramatic cash exit from a company (however you fancy up the accounting as a "restructuring charge") and disrupts operations and key relationships (often with customers) in a way that takes two years to rebuild, classifies as a disaster. If it also alienates employees, deflects the company into being in the reorganization business, leaves it inflexible to respond to opportunities, and shatters accountability and responsibility (everything is blamed on the previous regime), it moves right up there with an earthquake. A big, nasty Japanese/Mexican type earthquake.

Then add to that the fact that reengineering doesn't usually work. Hey! You crash diet and guess what? The weight creeps back on.

> **A modern company *must* look dramatically different at the end of each decade if it is to survive.**

A modern company *must* look dramatically different at the end of each decade if it is to survive. But the key is to get there with a million small changes rather than the "big bang" solution.

This is not a soft option and requires two fundamental elements:

- Every day, every opportunity to evolve the organization should be reviewed. There's a lot of natural turbulence as people move, leave, get promoted/ transferred, etc. No position should be filled without the job description being tortured to find the real need, thereby initiating everyday zero budgeting of the organization.

- Evolve to a position where you only directly, internally, resource for your core competency. Most companies contract out catering without a second thought. Ditto advertising. So why not the mail room? Shoot! Why not procurement? Then why not accounting, (please!). Outsourcing just demands a different way of thinking, but you can get there by evolution. Pick off one or two areas a year, that's maybe 15 each decade.

Compare Africa and North America. Almost every aspect of life is wildly different in the two, yet these two lands were once joined.

Armed with its mission statement (so I understand), North America set off and doggedly moved an inch a year. Every year, it reviewed its position, and even if there was no obvious need, it moved its inch, and today we are an ocean apart, literally in distance and metaphorically in culture. The O. J. Simpson trial? I rest my case.

In the interests of this project, I have researched accounting records for continental drift during the last few million years. These dramatic changes were achieved without *one* restructuring charge being taken to the accounts.

Organizational Excellence

Pass me the envelope, please

A couple of years ago those fine folks at the *Miami Herald* asked me to give the keynote speech at its Company of the Year Awards luncheon.

I agreed, although with some trepidation; these events are very tightly organized and timed, and it has become difficult for me in recent years to commit to tightly timed speeches because of the spontaneous roars of approval, impromptu standing ovations, and not-infrequent Mexican Waves that generally accompany my Billy Graham–type corporate sermons.

This one turned out to be no different, and I confess I got carried away. It's fair to say that, among the general scenes of bedlam during my speech—with grown men seen to be weeping and fine women mistaking me for Tom Jones and throwing items of rather intimate apparel at the stage—I lost my inborn sense of dignity and drifted from my carefully prepared speech.

I told my audience that, to be a serious candidate for such an award, a company needs to forget about profits or earnings per share, forget all about this feel-good, liberal, "nice place to work" drivel, and concentrate on the only thing that matters.

Integrity, integrity, integrity.

And (with apologies, I think, to Groucho Marx for stealing his line), once you have learned to fake that, you're in with a real chance.

It might have been OK if I'd quit there. The chairman might have made a full recovery. But there was no holding me back. I told them not to stop there, but go on to seek the personal accolade of Leader of the Year and, again, my advice was clear and helpful: As soon as you are appointed leader of anything you should move quickly (the same day if possible) to identify a possible successor to yourself.

And then fire the bastard.

The place erupted, and it was only as I was taking my fifth or sixth bow amidst the frenzy that I remembered I was only two places away from a bishop on the top table.

Luckily, my strategically placed spin-doctors in the audience told me afterward that he managed a wry smile, albeit with his eyes rolling and pointing upward.

I was surprised, therefore, when the new-generation *Herald Business* team asked me to take time to write in celebration of the event.

Times, of course, have changed dramatically since my speech. In that year it was safe to say that the world was becoming increasingly sickly, with the violent threatening to take over the peaceful, the irrational superseding the rational, and the superficial taking over from the substantial.

All that has changed, of course, and the world is now clearly clinically insane. Just witness some recent news items:

- The federal building in Oklahoma City is bombed. Hundreds die. A class action is taken out against the chemical company that made the fertilizer that some fruitcake then used in making a bomb.
- In Japan, a society now known (rather embarrassingly so to the West) as orderly and nonviolent is shaken by some hero emptying nerve gas down the subway.
- In Singapore a rogue trader hilariously brings down the Queen of England's bank. Rather more seriously, he illustrates that capitalism is now underpinned by about $16 *trillion* invested in derivatives that few people seem to be able to value and account for correctly.
- Back in the U.S., Bob Dole, a seemingly sanguine and viable presidential candidate, proposes America's least needed piece of legislation: the ability for everybody to buy automatic weapons again. Ain't that great?

> What becomes critical is that we find and highlight beacons of hope— isolated examples of sanity, values, and excellence— and try to learn from them.

It's a world in which there seems to be no hope, but we all know it will struggle on, somehow. What becomes critical, in that sort of script, is that we regularly find and highlight beacons of hope— isolated examples of sanity, values, and excellence—and try to learn from them.

In searching for a corporate example, the process itself is important—in that the choice is made by people without vested interests. Try reading annual reports of most Western companies, and you'll find thousands of shoo-ins for the next Company of the Year—companies that feature unqualified trading success, pursue nothing but excellence, have no structural problems, and treat their people real nice. Pass the sick bag.

So what does it take to be Company of the Year? Is it to be judged by traditional capitalist success criteria: stock trading at a multiple of 25 times earnings? Double digit growth in earnings per share every year? Big profits? Big market share?

Or do we bring into play criteria from the new liberalism: nice folks to work for? Lots of cultural diversity workshops? Day care for the employees' kids? Toilets for the disabled *before the law required them*?

My personal criteria have become a complex mix of all of these, expressed simply.

I don't think you can have a valid candidate that isn't commercially successful, although I would happily trade short-term fireworks for evidence of sustainability. But I also believe that *what* you achieve can only be part of the story today and that *how* you achieve success is just as important.

> **What** you achieve can only be a part of the story today. **How** you achieve success is just as important.

They represent the intangible style factors for a business and are all about *relationships*—how you relate to your employees, vendors, agents, distributors, and stockholders. And how you relate to the community or communities you work in and to the planet you temporarily occupy. I express such a complex concept simply: If it's a genuinely great company I'd like my *kids* to work there.

If you haven't got kids, substitute somebody else you care about and intend to care about in the future.

Success is important, but so is the ability for a company to understand that modern business involves thousands of relationships, designed and worked on so that each may flourish for the optimization of the individual *and the whole.* The really great companies realize that success comes because of that, not in spite of it.

Congratulations to any company that gets such an award. It will have deserved it. And good luck, because such an accolade brings responsibility in this bleak world. Such companies are beacons in a world where the light is fading fast. That's a tough job.

5

Doing Things Differently

Or maybe, doing different things

Introduction

It is now more than 35 years—and a quarter of a million printings— since Theodore Levitt wrote *Marketing Myopia* for the *Harvard Business Review.* It changed the minds of a generation about growth and success in business.

As the pace of change—particularly in technology and geopolitics— accelerates, the message is as relevant today as ever. But the passage of time has made the real message a bit misty.

Folks tend to remember the bunch of examples Levitt used to illustrate his point. The railways floundered because they thought they were in the railway industry when they were really in the transportation business. Hollywood slumped because it was convinced it was in the movie business and not popular entertainment. If they'd gotten it right, the railways would have developed cars and planes, and Hollywood would have invented television.

Fine. My copy of Levitt's thesis is nearly worn out. I can't tell you how many times I've discussed with my shaving mirror the fact Burger King is not in the hamburger business, but the cheap lunch industry. Or some such. These fascinating debates miss Levitt's real point: *There are no growth industries. There are only companies that capitalize on growth opportunities.*

Who am I to paraphrase the great man, but he might just as well have said that there are only growth-minded *people.*

The vision and the strength of mind necessary to challenge the ascendancy of an industry like the railways at the time of its peak are scary. To follow up the challenge with a proposal to develop an entirely new, untried, idea to figure out what came next was beyond the scope of anyone in it at the time. Frankly I don't see many examples happening on that scale today.

But on a lesser scale, it abounds every day and is present in most winners in business.

There are two pieces of logic I have never accepted:

- Let's do this because we've *always* done it this way.

- Let's not do this because we've *never* done it this way.

Change for change's sake is wrong. But when it's due and when it's right, it is the life blood of growth and success in business. It does not have to be about a dramatic shift in the core competency of your business. It can be about doing things differently just as much as doing different things.

Let me give you an example whose time has come. Many organizations have a big corporate headquarters building, usually downtown in a city. It is a long way from where the people live. It is stupidly expensive. It has thousands of little cubicles and cells where employees go about their "work." Some cells occupied by people called "officers" are very big and have Italian furniture and a secretary outside. She still types letters, albeit on several thousand dollars worth of word processor.

> Change for change's sake is wrong. But when it's due and when it's right it is the life blood of growth and success in business.

At the end of their dynasty, many dinosaurs had so evolved that they were inappropriate to what was happening on the planet. The only way many of them could stay alive and upright was to stand in water. That's as good a definition as any for the headquarters I described.

Changes in communication technology, the needs of the job, and the needs of the work force have been such that, if you were starting from scratch it would be the *last* model you would come up with. Yet they still exist. Even worse, they are still being built.

Starting from scratch *mentally* is the key; it requires a mind that constantly zero-budgets everything, a mind that faces everything with the ingoing thought: "If I hadn't done this before, how would I go about it?"

If the answer is that you would do it differently, then doing it differently must become the task at hand. Anything else is a weak compromise and will be a losing game plan.

Sometimes, of course, this zero-budget approach throws a real curve ball at you. Because the answer that comes back is that you wouldn't actually do it *at all.* It may be that it is a part of your business that you need to exit or that the task is better done by somebody else.

The challenge is the same in principle. Only this time it is about doing different things.

Try it on your own, mentally at first. My bet is that the way your company handles its information systems strategy suddenly looks daft. The routine meetings that take up such a chunk of your day begin to look dangerously useless. You might suddenly want to tear up all your contracts of employment and start again.

You might even decide that you could make the workplace fun. But that's right up there with moving from railways to airplanes on the scale of change needed for most organizations. Most require you to hang up your smile on a peg by the door as you come in. Leadership by grimace is the order of things.

The last six essays give you some ideas. The potential list of topics is endless.

27

Information Systems

And why I may be beheaded

I believe I am the only living Englishman between the ages of 30 and 50 who is not currently famous for having an affair with a female member of the British royal family.

That situation is about to change, because I am here in Monte Carlo to celebrate the launch of my new book, *The Queen and I: Our Forbidden Love.* This tells the tale of my torrid, tempestuous affair with Elizabeth during the last 15 years.

I am doing this for purely altruistic reasons, you understand, although I have accepted a small advance of 70 million Swiss Francs from one of the more acceptable London tabloids, the *Daily Groin.*

This literary masterpiece would have been impossible, of course, without my laptop PC. To write a book of such stature and dovetail it in with my jet-setting, *corps diplomatiques* lifestyle needs instant access to Windows and WordPerfect in the airport first class lounges and Admirals Clubs of the world.

All of that keyboarding got me to thinking about how computers have changed our lives—and the even more dramatic way they they have changed business. (Author's factoid: Buy a birthday card that plays "Happy Birthday" when you open it, and you are holding in your hand more computer power than existed *on earth* on the day I was born. And I agree, there are a number of different ways you can look at that fact.)

What are you going to be holding in your hand by Hallmark 50 years from now? Please don't answer that in front of the children.

In this progress-crazy world, we need an effective approach to systems for business, and let me first be brave enough to outline one for the planet.

Starting now, the principal of any school on earth who has access to electricity and any resources (money), and who allows pupils to leave school unable to log on a computer and/or word process their papers, should be taken out and shot. They should be revived, then shot again if those same pupils know a word of Latin.

Companies have already spent gillions on systems, of course, but my feeling is that we've run into a bit of a problem. Huge investments have been made against what I call supply-side strategies: A center of excellence team from the corporate Information Technology department arrives, develops, and implements them.

Obviously users are consulted, involved, and "trained" to use them and benefit accordingly. But as systems move away from the big central processor/utility approach toward desktop workstations, this way of doing things leaves a lot of problems, notably:

- The users are the ones who understand the business, but they still don't *think* in terms of systems when they consider their business problems/opportunities. As a result, we have unprofessional users.

- Supply-side thinking measures dumb things like "percentage of revenues spent on systems compared to our competitors." They do not measure percentage spent on *training* users (compared to competitors). In my view one is irrelevant amd the other highly relevant. You go figure.

- Leaders in supply-side-thinking companies are usually poor examples for the New Age company. These are the guys who still dictate one-line memos to secretaries who, in turn, type them up and then mail *and* fax them. I've known this to happen within the same building (honest).

- History is littered with supply-side systems initiatives being implemented, but then falling off in use and effectiveness when the central team moves on to something else. There's no demand pull to sustain it.

- A kind of duplicate system grows that is disk based and desk based. The underutility of the world's PC-based desktop publishing is estimated by me to be 96.51 percent.

My system strategy for business is as simple as murdering errant school principals was for the planet.

Technology generations now occur about every 18 months or so, so *miss the next one out.* The one after that will be cheaper and better, so use the money you save for a massive, comprehensive training effort to get the best return from what you have now and create a genuine cadre of professional users in your business.

Two-finger word processing, hit-and-miss e-mail, and the occasional Mickey Mouse spreadsheet do not qualify as a competitive edge any more. Start your training by overhauling your reluctant, Luddite, still-dictating leaders; if they don't comply, take them out, and shoot them as well. (Don't you wish.)

> **T**wo-finger word processing, hit-and-miss e-mail, and the occasional Mickey Mouse spreadsheet do not qualify as a competitive edge any more.

Yeah, OK! I'm in a bad mood. I'm negotiating a film deal for my new kiss-and-tell book. Although we've secured Whoopi Goldberg for the part of the Queen (we have to think of the American market), Harrison Ford is holding out for more money to play me.

And he'd be so perfect in the role. That chin . . .

As we dance jauntily along the information highway of the future, I want you to remember two things: The Titanic was faster than the iceberg, and Bill Gates is one of the richest men on earth. Study a picture of him and keep repeating that second point. Then I strongly advise you reach for a gin and tonic.

28

On Communication

And the strange case of the Kleenex box

I am at one with the sciences.

This may come as a surprise to some of you who know me (and here I must talk of my more superficial friendships) and who have seen me stare thoughtfully at a car for several minutes trying to figure out which end holds the engine.

And who have seen me examine a Kleenex box for even longer, searching for the battery. Hey! You pull one tissue out, and another one pops up. That needs electricity; trust me.

Misguided images of me indeed.

I could, and should, have been one of the scientific greats, but it's true that I drifted when failing, by a whisker, to get the Best Supporting Scientist Nobel Prize in

1952 for my early work in genetic architecture. Eventually, and ironically of course, this led to the magnificent recent breakthrough with the quark.

I recovered enough from that setback to help the immortal Dr. Jacob Bronowski write his astonishing opus, *The Ascent of Man,* in the 1970s. I was working with him at the Salk Institute on the sequel, *The Ascent of Man II: So What Happened to the Male Kennedys?* at his untimely death.

Which brings me to the topic for this essay: Communication. Gurus began to write about it a lot about 20 years ago, at about the same time that corporate leaders began to understand that their communication skills were Neanderthal. These two facts are linked.

About the same time, I began to be unhappy with the word *communication* because it seemed so inadequate to reflect what was actually taking place. But it was some time before I found a better definition, and I owe it all to my deep scientific background.

For nearly 20 years I had been some sort of an industrial-strength company doctor, going into companies where morale was low or nonexistent. So too, usually, was investment. Performance was in the toilet. Everything and everybody seemed frozen. In one spectacular case, which shall be nameless, all of the above applied. On each occasion, the atmosphere could be likened to the classic physical phenomenon: the vacuum.

Late one night, armed only with the most basic scientific apparatus (a six-pack), I let my mind wander on the subject. I remembered from my musings with Bronowski how air rushes in to fill a vacuum, and I reasoned that if I didn't fill the vacuum with good, positive air, there would be many who would go with negative air. These naysayers, rumormongers, and advanced corrosion artists are to be found by the water fountains in most organizations.

The challenge was one of communication all right, but here's where I began to understand why the word had become so inadequate. Throughout history, all successful communication mechanisms and processes had been equally capable of *receiving* as well as transmitting information. This principle applied to smoke signals, mirrors, and Morse code—also to flags, voice mail, and magnets on the fridge door.

But it didn't seem to apply to business. Communication had come to mean "tell or give out" and not to "listen or receive."

Immediately, communication became *vacuum management* in my mind.

The key to its effective management is to understand, first, that it is about process and not content. Second, that communication is not just about crisis management but a day-to-day challenge in times when the preposterous pace of change forces a company to leave a vacuum behind it as it responds quickly. Or dies.

I remember doodling a lyric a few years back with Cat Stevens before he went off to find himself. Somewhere in that glorious song "Father and Son" is the line:

Ever since I could talk I've been told that I must listen.

And is that ever true in business.

People want information, but they want the leaders to know their views as well. This drive is based not just on how information affects them, but because they can *contribute* to solving a company's problems and taking advantage of opportunities. And because sometimes people need to *challenge*. If your company's culture doesn't relish challenge and allow for it, quit now.

> "Ever since I could talk I've been told that I must listen."

Hey, I've just remembered that old Cat never credited me on the album! Ah, well. I had plenty of spiritual reward.

A rule of thumb I have applied to vacuum management is 50:50. Half your efforts consist of giving information out, half receiving and digesting it. And don't just limit your efforts to any one stakeholder in the organization. It's valid for all of them. It's a tough challenge to keep information channels up because it's so much easier to dole out carefully selected bits of information to selected audiences and then hide. (Witness most annual reports.) But if you do hide, the vacuum stays unmanaged and the corrosion merchants wreak havoc.

For once, modern electronic communication devices such as e-mail and voice mail can help. In one business I put a weekly 5-to-10-minute communal e-mail out on all sorts of bits and pieces affecting the business. It had both serious and light subject matter and I got between 50 and 100 *personal* replies back. In the science of vacuum management, that's gold dust.

I tried to keep to the 50:50 rule and often found it just wasn't enough listening. Then I figured out another formula: you have two eyes, two ears, and one mouth, which is four organs to receive, one to give out information. I tried that ratio. It works better.

But 20 years later the "communicators" are still out there, talking away, failing to manage the vacuum, missing the point, and shooting themselves in the Gucci loafers. Why? Why would they do that? I'm here to tell you it remains one of life's mysteries.

A bit like the Kleenex box, really.

29

What Happened to My Job?

Do you believe in magic?

Twenty-five years ago John Sebastian and I electrified a generation with our duet at Woodstock. Little did we know that we were signaling the end of something fundamental for the old world of business. Sure, we captured the *zeitgeist* of the time as we sang, as if with one voice, "The Flowers in Our Hair Are Blowin' in the Winds of Change," but something was never goin' to be the same again.

It was the need *to be there.*

Before you accuse me of inhalin' illegal substances (*moi?*), let me explain.

Years later Frank Sinatra recorded an album of duets with a series of famous vocalists. He never physically shared a studio with most of them. Nat King Cole harmonized with his daughter and appeared on video with her some years after his death. Today, a doctor conducts detailed laser surgery on a patient, by electronic linkup, from a facility in a different time zone. Forrest Gump (filmed 1994) converses on screen with President Kennedy (who died in 1963).

What's going on here? And what are the implications for business?

Everybody grew up understanding what a "job" was. Most companies were built on a collection of them, and they were the cornerstone of a working person's life. Sure, the traveling salesperson traveled and lots of jobs entailed moving around a bit, but by and large you got out of bed, went somewhere familiar, did something familiar, returned home, added a teaspoonful of something called "private life," and went to bed. And then got up and repeated same, hopefully until you were well into your sixties.

It was an acceptable relationship between an organization and an employee. Kinda imperfect, but it seemed to work. But it worked because the needs of the company were one-dimensional, as were the needs of the employee. At least that's what they both thought, and it was domestic or corporate heresy to think otherwise. But even if they had thought differently, no tools existed to help anyone do much about it.

Times, they aren't a-changin' any more. They've changed.

Look at it first from the company's point of view. Most have invested in technology—production, information systems, and so on—and they need to get full use out of that investment to justify the cost. Full use is not 8:30 A.M. to 5:00 P.M.

In addition, the interests of many businesses now run across time zones inside the U.S., European, Pacific Rim, or South American theaters—in some cases all of them.

Frequently customers need support, or employees need to network, 24 hours a day.

Even the jobs themselves are no longer consistent over time. Almost every job will vary dramatically in skill and/or input required during the course of, say, a year. The needs during the planning cycle, for example, differ from those during a big sales push. Projects, internal to the department or linking up with others, come and go. Organizational development *continually* brings changes. There's really nothing left that needs somebody to turn up somewhere and repeat and repeat and repeat . . .

What of the other side of the equation? The employee? Many companies today genuinely seek the benefits of "diversity"—with the dual goals of a more healthy and productive atmosphere. Some pay lip service to the idea; others have made real progress and have genuinely benefitted. Few have taken it on to where it can now go: a whole new series of relationships inside the organization.

Just as business can no longer define a single job that is one-dimensional, neither can the work force offer a single person who is so limited. Life patterns and styles have evolved to a degree that no two people want the same thing out of anything, most of all their employment. Some employees want part time; others want 80 hours a week. Some like early mornings, some days, some nights. Some would love three months off a year; some would hate it. Some would have no problem with their work-place being a station they take over from somebody else at 5:00 P.M.; others need personal territory that they lock up and that stays dark till they get back. (These are generally called "officers.") Some folks even believe they can work better from home.

Now, remember Frank Sinatra, Nat King Cole, and the surgeon?

Add to the plethora of possible working patterns the fact that technology has developed to the level that, even for the most complex of tasks, you don't always have to be there. Multimedia PCs, e-mail, voice mail, fax machines, beepers, conference calling, and teleconferencing are all widespread today. In fact they fall pretty low on the technology scale. They offer huge opportunities for remote, even home, basing for the task at hand.

The "job" as we knew it is dead, and I for one will not mourn its passing. But it is a mind-blowing opportunity for the enlightened business and its people. I figure that a company that matches its own multidimensional needs with those of its people, and creates a collection of a whole new style of relationships, is going to take what it wants and leave the rest behind, floundering.

And all that came from a spontaneous, unrehearsed "happening" with John and me 25 years ago—amazing.

This year Woodstock celebrated the Twenty-Fifth Anniversary of the Mudfest with another concert. Would you believe that, this time, each field toilet was equipped with its own air freshener spray? Of course you wouldn't.

30

Office Design

And the attractions
of shrimping

Do you have depressing days? Days when you stop and reflect that the world's been going steadily downhill since you were born, and you may well have been a factor?

I was in England recently, working on a project to help Hugh Grant ruin his image, and I picked up a copy of the new *Chambers Encyclopaedic English Dictionary*. This is a two-million word compendium that has just been published.

The new words, reflecting the planet's progress (progress?) during the last few decades are truly disturbing, and in the interests of filling up space, I list a small sample: *date rape, carjacking, ethnic cleansing, fetal alcohol syndrome, white knuckle*, and *sexploitation*. These are just a few of the nightmarish new entries, offset only occasionally by a flash of genuine late-twentieth-century cause for celebration such as *shrimping* (the practice of sucking one's partner's toes, courtesy of Princess Fergie). Welcome to the age of the porno-Royals.

Casting my mind forward, I wondered what the new words will be in, say, the year 2010.

I forecast that *hotdesking* will be there for certain, spelling the end of personal territory in the office building. I'm surprised it didn't make it this time. Must've been a close one.

The evolution, design, and occupation of office space in the twentieth-century corporation has had little to do with business needs and much more to do with those little idiosyncrasies of the male species that make us so attractive.

Similar ones involve a need to zap the TV every 2.38 seconds, a refusal to stop the car to ask directions when lost, a need to spread the three remaining hairs from ear to shining ear across a bald head, and a deep love of cheese that comes out of a tin.

Let me be quite clear here. Women would have evolved the science of design differently, and they increasingly do as they thankfully exert more influence in modern companies. But office design and occupation has been a male thing, and the results are, to a degree, predictable.

It is essentially a hierarchical science. The first rule is that the most senior person, who is therefore away from the office the *most*, gets the biggest office with the best view and light. The pond scum, who are there all day, every day, get the cubicles that face the boiler.

There is also a need to infest the office with assorted artifacts, designed to give off a carefully chosen set of optic signals to the casual onlooker:

- The first signal is that the incumbent was, and probably *still could be*, a pretty good sportsman (witness mounted team photographs, sports caps, etc.).
- He moves in the right circles (photograph with Lee Iacocca, H. Ross Perot, etc.).

- He reads a lot of serious stuff (couple of bookcases of impressive hardbacks—mostly without the pages slit).
- You're talking about a man of family values here, pal (photo of wife, or wives, and several of the children). The last items also have the practical role of reminding him what they look like and possibly their names.

I joined Shell Oil in England, in 1969. I was the first of a generation of university graduates who didn't have to carry a hat and gloves while on business, but that's another essay. The office system defied belief even then, as it surely must now.

You started with a desk, which had one drawer, facing your buddy, with four desks to a room. And when you got promoted? You got three drawers down one side of the desk. Promoted again? A piece of glass for the desktop. Again? A piece of green felt cloth to go under the glass. Again? DA-DA! Only two of you to a room. Again? Tea on a tray at your desk, not from the trolley in the corridor. Again? A filing drawer in the other side of your desk. Again? Your own office. Then a desk plus a coffee table and two casual chairs. Again? I dunno. I'd long gone.

It may seem too bizarre for words, but much of that thinking is still around today in various disguises (see also: company car policies).

It is all over now, guys. And mourn it not. High-tech workstations, the ability to do much of your job from anywhere on earth via modern communication technology, coupled with high rents in prime office locations, now outlaw the dumb use of space. An office I knew in London cost $125 per square foot to rent. I remember looking at a waste paper bin and working out the rent for the floor underneath it. Ouch!! Pricey.

Office status and privilege have, at long last, been shown to be largely counterproductive, and a new office design mentality is emerging. It is increasingly asexual and efficient.

It is beginning to look something like an Admirals Club, with lots of workstations, groups of two, three, or four seats, bookable meeting rooms and bookable private interview rooms. A constant supply of coffee is on hand, together with soft drinks and light snacks on a long table at the side. Everbody has his or her own phone/fax/copier/ access codes and an appropriate PC.

> **Office status and privilege have, at long last, been shown to be largely counterproductive.**

And *hotdesking* has arrived. When you finish with a workstation, somebody else uses it.

So, how about another new word for the year 2010? I forecast that the word *brand-defense* will enter popular vocabulary, defined as the practice of big brands sponsoring the legal defense for megastars accused of murder.

I do not forecast that these will be the big successful brands—the Nikes and Coca Colas of the year 2010—but those who've had their day, missed their chances, and need to gamble. Watch out for Dominos and KFC in this category.

OK, altogether now. Conjugate the verb *to shrimp*.

31

On Meetings

Whaddya mean, do some work?

Looking back, it was an honor, but it didn't seem so at the time.

In 1989 I was asked to be both chairperson and secretary to the biggest meeting in the history of the world (and probably the universe): the Kumbh Mela, which takes place in India at the point where the Ganges and Jamuna rivers converge.

The main agenda is to celebrate the creation myths of Hinduism and, in particular, the awakening of Brahma the creator. The devotees meet to wash away their sins in these most sacred of rivers.

Satellite photographs were able to estimate that close to 15 million people assembled that day, and they also recorded my venerable efforts to run the meeting. I made sure it moved forward at a purposeful pace, that apologies for absence were noted, that tactical action plans were agreed upon, and that detailed minutes were recorded and distributed. It was my triumph in bringing order out of the chaos (called "masterful" by the *Calcutta Herald*'s Business Monday section) that won me my reputation as the guru of the business meeting.

It was a skill I found I needed to use to the fullest back in the West.

A few years ago, my youngest son, seeing me doing paperwork at home late one night, asked if it wouldn't be a better script all round if I worked when I was at work, and familied when I was with the family. I told him, lovingly, that I too would like that, but it was not possible because work was *where you went to meetings.* Actual work was, therefore, something you had to do someplace else.

In the few years since then, two things have happened: My son has perfected the art of being a negative cash-flow family unit, and the situation with meetings has become worse—dramatically so.

Most meetings are unnecessary, many of them pointless, and pretty much all of them are badly organized. A lot of them hinder, rather than help, the business process.

Of course there is a need to meet in the normal course of business. Despite the advent of modern electronic and computerized communications, there is, on occasion, a need for two or more people to physically get together to do some things. But so often when people do meet, the first thing they realize is that whatever it is they are meeting about would have been better handled by one of the other processes. Of course, they don't tell each other that.

Too often people meet without knowing and *agreeing* to what end a particular meeting is a means (the purpose of getting together). And let me raise my voice here, folks, and tell you that the fact it is a Monday, at 10 A.M., is spectacularly *not* a purpose to hold a meeting.

There are only three possible reasons to meet: to give information, to debate options, or to decide something.

It is which of these, or which combination of these, you agree to beforehand that makes the difference in the effectiveness of the process. It helps—to the degree that I believe makes it essential—when one person is appointed to "own" the meeting, with the jobs of determining beforehand what the purpose is and of telling everybody.

Giving information is the weakest purpose of the three and, as you might therefore expect, it is the most commonly used because it can usually be done more effectively another way. Getting people together to listen to a presentation is dumb because everyone's ability to digest information differs. It is a much more productive use of available common time to debate or decide things.

> There are only three possible reasons to meet: to give information, to debate options, or to decide something.

It's far better to give information out beforehand. Remember: Even the most sophisticated reports and presentations can now go out via e-mail or disk, and folks can then digest it at their own pace. If you do give out information at a meeting, tell those present exactly what you're doing so they know that nothing is expected of them.

A debate needs an owner, or at least a facilitator, who has the responsibility to provide information on the options beforehand, together with appropriate projections, upsides, and downsides. And a preferred course. In any process, it is usually critical for you to get input from other people before you recommend or make a final decision—in particular from those who will be affected and/or those who are wiser than you in specific areas. Sometimes the discussion itself can lead to an additional (better) option than any of those listed at the outset.

By far the most important reason to meet is to *decide something.* For this to work everybody present must understand and agree precisely what has been decided before the meeting concludes. Time and again, when a decision has been made, a quick poll of those present will show subtle variations on what has actually been perceived to have been agreed, and the variations usually are directly related to the interests of those polled.

When I "owned" a meeting, my approach was simple. If somebody wanted a decision, I asked them to write me a three-line summary of the exact decision required, which I sent out before the meeting. This would tell the delegates exactly what would be recorded afterward unless we agreed to make changes.

What are the Golden Rules for meetings? First, there is, today, an understandable hatred of unnecessary bureaucracy, the administrative cholesterol of business. Copious minutes of meetings that wait to be approved (rewritten?) by the chairperson and that are then distributed two weeks after the event are a facile example of this science at its worst. But a short (maximum of one page) set of agreed action/review notes, put on voice mail or e-mail the same day, is essential.

> **Don't try and flick a decision through an "information-giving" process. It is naughty.**

Golden Rule Number 2? Don't try and flick a decision through an "information-giving" process. It is naughty.

Final rule? Do all of the techniques I've advocated and then *don't provide seats* in the meeting room.

I'm serious.

Humor in the Workplace

Hey, be careful with that thing

I get depressed so easily these days.

I get upset, for instance, when I think of Wham splitting up. I get distraught when I think about how Emma Thompson and Kenneth Brannagh (buddies of mine when we were rookies together in the Royal Shakespeare Company) have become such unattractive people since fame overtook them.

And I'm beyond Prozac when I despair for the funding needs of public broadcasting.

When I'm in these depressions, however, I always have a remedy at hand: Take time out and think of the five moments in life when I laughed the most. And then I rank them in ascending order. Sometimes a couple of different ones creep into the five, but one is always present and it always wins.

It happened when I was 16, in South Africa, staying with my childhood buddy Nelson Mandela.

Our people were the Xhosa, and the local regent decided it was time for us both to become men. We were to be formally incorporated into society. A lengthy and elaborate ritual, lasting two full days, was involved— preceded by a long journey to the mystic Tyhalara on the banks of the Mbeshe River. It then included feasts, daring exploits, and storytelling before the magnificent ceremony itself.

I remember feeling a little nervous as the *Ingcibi* approached us, rehearsing as I was the cry of *"Ndiyindoda"* ("I am a man!") that I must make at the crucial moment. I held my breath, seeking the inner strength I would surely need. Then it happened. With one motion of his *assegai,* I was circumcised.

Nelson, of course, was very brave and correct. He barely flinched. I think I shouted the right word. I certainly shouted something. But then I remember nothing but laughter for several minutes—maybe hours, possibly days—afterward.

Such fun—and it occurred to me recently that we have so few of such laughter-fests in modern business today. Can humor exist at all in the modern workplace? Is there any role for a grin in the miserable, splenetic, stressed-out, decaying *mal du siecle* that is today's corporate life?

Of course there is, partly for the simple reason that we have no choice. If the great director in the sky pressed the freeze-frame button on a million occasions in an ordinary working day across the business world there would be enough unplanned comic material to make Sting lighten up.

In 1977 I was appointed leader of a small party of engineers to visit Tokyo to complete the acquisition of several million dollars worth of computerized warehousing systems. Big stuff. I was a *wunderkind* at the time and took my responsibilities seriously, researching all the complex business and social intricacies needed for a successful visit to Japan. Including the giving and receiving of token gifts each time you met someone new.

Very thoughtfully, we had a bag full of such presents and many sheets of paper in which to wrap them. We did not wrap them before the journey in case any customs officials wanted to inspect them, so shortly after our arrival, we assembled in my hotel room to do the job.

I do not normally stereotype people. I never glibly attribute set characteristics to any one gender, race, or group. But I will tell you this now: White males cannot wrap presents neatly.

The sight of my bed after a frustrating hour or so was nothing short of hilarious. Which turned into an 11-day fit of uncontrollable giggling as, time after time, we received gifts wrapped by somebody who was obviously a black belt in origami and gave something in return that looked like it had been put together by 4077 M*A*S*H*.

And this humor occurred without the distraction of one of the engineers becoming dramatically constipated, and (with the rest of us watching intently from behind a display of shampoo) describing his problem to a local drug store assistant in *sign language.*

Comedy abounds in business every day, you can't prevent it. If you can stand back from it, recognize it, and somehow harness it, it offers a huge opportunity to lighten the journey and to make for a more relaxed (and productive?) work force.

If humor doesn't happen naturally, you can, and should, create your own, but there are a couple of no-go areas to avoid. First, there is a difference between using humor to lighten the working day and being frivolous with people's lives, careers, and investments—and if you don't understand the difference you shouldn't be in charge of a dog pound. One is nutritional, one corrosive.

Second rule: There is a time and place for a light touch. Firing people (or, sometimes worse, telling them they have not got the job they've been dreaming about and relying on) is not the time to run through your famous Jerry Lewis impersonation (unless you run the French Division).

> There is a difference between using humor to lighten the working day and being frivolous with people's lives, careers, and investments.

But do try to introduce some appropriate fun. Even if you are one of the new breed of corporate leaders and were trained for the mission by having your sense of humor surgically removed at birth, plug a smile into whatever communication techniques you use to talk and listen with your people, be they a small team or a mighty corporation. Particularly if it is at your own expense. Even more so if you can do it at the expense of your own dignity and humbug.

Voice mail is great for this; remember, you've spent thousands of dollars on it, and it would be great to get something more out of it than just an expensive answering machine. It is obvious good form to stay away from controversy and cheap shots, but remember that politically correct fun is an oxymoron, so take some small risks.

Look around you. All is lost. We are clearly living in the last days of the planet. But my steadfast belief is that it would be stylish to smile as we implode back into the rain forest or explode up and out through the hole in the ozone layer caused by Julio Inglesias' hair spray.

Only joking. There you go.

Index

Other books of interest to you from Irwin Professional Publishing . . .

THE PARADOX PRINCIPLES

How High Performance Companies Manage Chaos and Contradictions to Achieve Superior Results

The Price Waterhouse LLP Change Integration Team

The *Paradox Principles* shows managers how to face those conflicts and use paradox as a dynamic tool to create balance and focus within an organization. Lessons learned from executives at over 200 high performance companies and the collective experience of the Price Waterhouse Change Integration Team show managers how to achieve unparalleled success by better managing the paradoxes inherent in their industry, organization, and strategy.

0-7863-0499-5   250 pages

NOT JUST FOR CEOS

Sure Fire Success Secrets for All of Us

John H. Zenger

Offers practical guidelines and tips for the behavior required to succeed in today's business. While based on the latest research, the suggestions are expressed in practical terms easily understood by everyone in the organization.

0-7863-0528-2   188 pages

THE LEADER'S EDGE

Mastering the 5 Skills of Breakthrough Thinking

Guy Hale

Written by Guy Hale, founder and CEO of Alamo Learning Systems, *The Leader's Edge* provides the tools to master the "art" of thinking as well as the

(Continued)

confidence to handle any business decision. Providing practical skills rather than philosophy alone, *The Leader's Edge* instructs readers on the five skills needed to think more accurately.

0-7863-0426-X   190 pages

BOOM

Visions and Insights for Creating Wealth in the 21st Century

Frank Vogl & James Sinclair

"An important contribution to the understanding of an increasingly competitive global economy."

**—Martin Sorrell
Chief Executive,
WPP Group plc**

Through *Boom,* internationally recognized experts Frank Vogl and James Sinclair show corporations how to best position themselves for the new era. The corporations that recognize this "boom" and build organizations that can take advantage of this huge global market will be well positioned for phenomenal growth and unlimited earning potential.

0-7863-0527-4   256 pages

GET BETTER OR GET BEATEN

31 Leadership Secrets from GE's Jack Welch

Robert Slater

This book examines 31 of those secrets in a fast-paced, easy-to-digest format that reads like a manager's "little instruction book." Includes the personal beliefs, bywords, principles, and techniques that helped Jack Welch become the most respected CEO in America.

0-7863-0235-6   160 pages

BETTER CHANGE

Best Practices for Transforming Your Organization

The Price Waterhouse Change Integration Team

Written for business leaders who understand that their company's prosperity depends on successful transformation, *Better Change* offers the insight and experience of some of the world's outstanding thought leaders on change, The Price Waterhouse Change Integration Team.

0-7863-0342-5   190 pages

Available in fine bookstores and libraries everywhere!